Rapture Revelation:
The Blessed Hope!

D1306180

Ann M. Rowan

www.flwi.org

Rapture Revelation: The Blessed Hope
By Ann Maria Rowan

Unless otherwise noted, the Scripture quotations are from
The King James Version of the Bible.

International Standard Book Numbers:
ISBN: 9798523622106

Printed in the United States of America

I dedicate this book to the Lord Jesus Christ who by His grace gave me a supernatural revelation of the future, and Who sovereignly revealed to me my need of salvation by grace through faith. I want to thank my family, who has supported me with love through the years.

Additionally, I want to dedicate this to Breanna Faith, my precious granddaughter. May she intimately know the One who loves her even more than "Nana" does...

Table of Contents

RAPTURE REVELATION:

I give little credence to many of the accounts of supposed "supernatural revelation" that I hear about. I don't believe in the sightings of the Virgin Mary's face being divinely imprinted onto a screen door, or that her image has been supernaturally molded on a bran muffin, or of supposed alien encounters, or a host of other "divine" or "paranormal" phenomena. Had I not personally experienced the following Divine visitation, I would have been skeptical about hearing of a young girl's apocalyptic "vision," and probably would have attributed it to a child's overly-active imagination. But I did experience it.

I certainly was not *looking* for a supernatural sign that day in 1971. As a typical, not-too-religious, Catholic twelve-year-old, I was playing outside in our quiet Burlington, Iowa neighborhood with my friend, Tia Cook. It was a sunny, summer day with a blue sky dotted with a few puffy, white clouds. I recall seeing the lush tree-lined horizon as one would look up the asphalt street toward the north. We were in her yard playing tetherball—monotonously hitting the ball and taking turns wrapping it around the pole. We were not talking about God or doing anything "religious." All of a sudden, literally out of the blue, I saw a vision. My eyes were wide open but I could not see the normal neighborhood surroundings. All that I could see was a 3-D movie-like vision of what I innately knew to be a Divine warning from God.

THE VISION

As I stood there transfixed on the scene before me, I tried to explain it to my friend, saying, "Tia... I'm seeing these things!" I began to relay to her the details of what was appearing before my eyes: I saw darkness and people in extreme fear, turmoil, confusion, and violence. People were hoarding food and anarchy seemed to reign... almost like the destruction and chaos after a major natural disaster with rioting and looting, only many times worse in scope and intensity. People were running and were absolutely terrified. One young lady's face in particular stands out. She was around thirty years old, with shoulder length, brown hair and had a look of total horror in her eyes—crazed horror. It was as if the people knew there was no escape out of the dark devastation they were facing. Many people were arming themselves with automatic submachine gun type weapons to protect themselves and their food supplies. Even the "good people" (respectable members of society) were engulfed in the mayhem. I recall seeing an older, mostly bald man in a dark business suit being very "trigger happy" with his gun, willing to kill to protect his food. Though I knew very little about God or the Bible, I knew that I had just witnessed the end of the world.

I don't recall how long it lasted... it could have been a minute or five minutes. *Tia would have been able to estimate better than I.* What I did know was that God had given me this vision and it was a warning of what was going to happen. I knew that it was of grave importance and that I needed to document what I had just seen. I wrote down all the details of the vision on a piece of paper, and at the end of the description I wrote: "If I ever think that this did not happen or that it was just my imagination, I will know that the devil stole it [the revelation] from me." Tia and I made multiple copies of the vision and both took several copies and hid them in various "safe" places, one being in my ballerina jewelry box. Several years later, after my family had moved to another state, I found a copy of the vision. At that time I was in a rebellious stage and doubted God's existence. When I saw the paper, I said, "How ridiculous!" and threw it away. I wish now that I had my paper to reference.

SO WHAT?

So, what significance did that "vision" have concerning the times that we are in now? The Bible states in Joel 2, in the last days before Jesus returns, there would be such supernatural signs from God: *"And it shall come to pass in the last days, says God, I will pour out of my Spirit upon all flesh: and your sons and **your daughters** shall prophesy, and your young men shall see **visions**, and your old men shall dream dreams: And on my servants and on my handmaidens I will pour out in those days of my Spirit; and they shall prophesy: **And I will show wonders in heaven above, and signs in the earth beneath**; blood, and fire, and vapor of smoke: The sun shall be turned into darkness, and the moon into blood, before that great and notable day of the Lord comes."*

In recent years, we have heard about the Mayan predictions of the end of the world in 2012, Biblical "harbingers" that seem to have been fulfilled in current events including 9-11, and a general interest in end of time prophecy. Multiple books and movies have featured Bible prophecy with all its foreboding, apocalyptic scenarios. A few misguided people have waited on mountain tops for Jesus to return on a certain day. When that day came and went without event, many have discounted anything that has to do with end-time prophecy.

However, if one would take an objective look at our society and world events, they must admit that "something" is happening. Look at the record breaking weather extremes—heat, cold, fires, snowfall, drought, flooding. Consider the significant increase in recent years of major natural disasters—not just in frequency, but in intensity. Where there used to be an occasional earthquake of note, of late there have been unprecedented, massive earthquakes. Look at the social degradation. Children come to school and kill other children. There's widespread gang violence, and general disrespect of authority. That which used to be taboo is accepted. There seems to be no restraint with abnormal and promiscuous sex... and it's publicly flaunted. It seems that our culture has lost its conscience. Look at the threats all over the world of terrorism and nuclear weapons in the hands of madmen. All of this, along with the current global political and economic upheavals, seems to indicate that some major changes are imminent.

BIBLE PROPHECY

According to Bible prophecy there is change coming, but it will not be good. There will be a global economic collapse, along with massive death and destruction. A centralized government with a multi-national "peace keeping" force will be set in place to bring peace out of the chaos. During that time billions of people will die. The Bible calls this the time of "great tribulation," also known as the "Day of the Lord." It is a time when God is going to allow judgment to fall upon the unrepentant inhabitants of the world. It is the time of His wrath.

In the midst of this very dark hour of human history, there is a bright hope. It is the Rapture of the Church. Jesus promised that He would come again and rescue His people from the earth before God's judgments fall.[1] The Bible teaches that when Jesus appears all true believers will be "caught up" into Heaven to be with the Lord. Only then God will pour out His judgments of wrath upon the earth. If this is true, then it is of utmost importance both to understand the Rapture, and to be prepared for it. Bible prophecy will very soon have a great impact on every one of us.

Before reading any further, you must determine whether or not you choose to believe Bible prophecy. If the Bible is just a collection of men's opinions and poetic sayings preserved for millennia, then what follows is just an exercise in semantics and religious ramblings of no real consequence. But if the Bible is the Divinely-inspired, Word of God that is assured to come to pass, then one would be wise to take careful heed to what it says.

---

[1] John 14:1-6, I Thessalonians 1:10

IS THE BIBLE TRUE?

The first consideration must be to determine whether or not the Holy Bible can be trusted to accurately foretell the future. We can look at the track record of the Scripture by considering the numerous prophecies that have already been fulfilled. In the Old Testament, there were many Messianic passages written hundreds of years before Jesus Christ that predicted exact and very minute details of His life. From His obscure birth in Bethlehem (Micah 5:2), travel to Egypt (Hosea 11:1), ministry in Galilee (Isaiah 9:1, 2), to His death on the cross at the hands of the Romans (Psalm 22:16, Daniel 9, Isaiah 53, Zechariah 12), Jesus completely fulfilled all the prophecies concerning His life, death, and resurrection. How could the prophets have known 500 years in advance that Jesus would be betrayed by a friend for 30 pieces of silver?[2] How could they predict almost one thousand years before the fact that Messiah would have His hands and feet pierced as a form of capital punishment--before crucifixion had even been invented? If there were just one or two specific prophecies fulfilled, one could perhaps attribute it to chance. However, over 300 exact predictions concerning Jesus Christ were fulfilled to the letter. The statistical probability of all of these prophecies being fulfilled in one man is 1 chance in 480 billion x 1 billion x 1 trillion—far beyond the realm of "chance."[3] Prophecies regarding Jesus Christ have been 100% accurate.

The accuracy of other Biblical predictions is just as compelling. Consider Ezekiel's prophecies concerning the dispersion and regathering of the Jews in the land of Israel. He predicted that Israel would be judged for their idolatry by being taken captive by their enemies and forced to serve them on foreign soil. A total of 430

---

[2] Psalm 41:9; Zechariah 11:12, 13
[3] Peter Stoner, Science Speaks, Chicago: Moody Press, 1969, 4)

years of judgment was determined upon the Jews. (See Ezekiel 4 in the Scripture Reference section.) If they would not repent after being punished by God, then the judgment (dominion by foreign entities) would be multiplied by seven.[4]

In 606 B.C. the Jews were taken captive by the Babylonians. For 70 years they served their enemies on foreign soil. Then, in 536 B.C., King Cyrus of Persia issued a royal edict that allowed the Jews to return to the land of Israel. (That king, by the way, was predicted *by name* over 200 years before the fact!)[5] When given the opportunity to return from the land of their captivity, most of the Jews refused. They preferred the idolatrous society in which they were entrenched to serving God in the Holy Land of Israel. Therefore, God multiplied the remaining 360 years of their judgment (being dominated by foreign powers) by seven, for a total of 2,520 more years.

A Bible year is 360 days.[6] If one calculates the Biblical years remaining into our solar year of 365.25 days, a total of 2,483.8 years remained before the Jew's judgment was complete. On May 14, 1948 (2,483.8 years later, as there is no year zero) the sovereign State of Israel was established. For the first time in over 2,500 years the Jews had a homeland and were not dominated by foreign entities. Ezekiel's prediction was fulfilled to the day!

Consider also the amazing writings of Daniel. Hundreds of years before the fact, he predicted the exact order of the world powers that would rise up after the Babylonian empire (the Medo-Persian, Greek, and Roman, and even the revived Roman Empire: the European Union.)[7] He was so accurate that he prophesied exact political alliances concerning Alexander the Great, his four generals

---

[4] Leviticus 26:15-18
[5] Isaiah 44:28
[6] Genesis 7:11, 24, 8:4
[7] Daniel chapters 2 & 7

and their territories, Cleopatra and the various intrigues of the political marriages, of Antiochus Epiphanes, and exactly how many days he would dominate the Jews' Temple.[8]

How could he predict 600+ years before the event the *exact time* when the Jew's Messiah, Jesus Christ, would be "cut off" (killed) by the Romans and how the destruction of the Jewish Temple would ensue?[9] These predictions were so detailed and accurate that they had to be supernaturally revealed. The discovery of the Dead Sea Scrolls proves these prophecies were written before these events— not "conveniently" afterwards.

These and many more examples in scripture validate that the Holy Bible is the inspired Word of God, and that it can be trusted regarding its predictions of future events. The Bible states: *"All scripture is given by inspiration of God"*[10] and *"prophecy came in old time by holy men of God who spoke as they were moved by the Holy Ghost."*[11] The Psalmist tells us: *"The law of the LORD is perfect, converting the soul: the testimony of the LORD is sure, making wise the simple...All Thy commandments are truth. Concerning Thy testimonies, I have known of old that Thou hast founded them forever...Thy word is true from the beginning."*[12] The Bible is the true, inspired, Word of the Lord. The prophecies concerning the end of the age will be fulfilled exactly as they are written.

---

[8] Daniel chapters 8 & 11
[9] Daniel 9:26
[10] II Timothy 3:16
[11] II Peter 1:21
[12] Psalm 16:7, Psalm 119:151

INTERPRETING THE BIBLE

Having established that Bible prophecy can be trusted is the first step. Then one must know how to interpret what is written. Some who are not fully acquainted with Holy Scripture may find *apparent* contradictions concerning different passages that they read. For instance, one can look at the account of Jesus' birth from both Matthew and Luke and think that there are inconsistencies. In one case the writer records that shepherds came to Jesus, and the other that Magi brought Him presents. Which is right? Both! Luke[13] describes when Jesus was first born, and Matthew[14] recounts what happened when Jesus was approximately 1½ years old. So, as with any doctrine of the Bible, one must include the FULL account of all that is written on that topic to get a complete and accurate understanding. This is especially true with Bible prophecy. One cannot disallow or "throw out" any scripture because you do not understand it or because it does not agree with your particular ideology.

As one reads Bible prophecy and attempts to decipher timelines and events, one may become confused if they fail to recognize that God's Word is "divided." In other words, there are segments of prophecy that are directed to a specific audience for a specific time. Not all prophetic scripture applies to everyone. For instance, Jesus prophesied to the Jews living in the first century regarding the destruction of Herod's Temple in Luke 21:5, which came to pass exactly as predicted forty years later. Further on in the same chapter He prophesied of the end-time signs that we see now.[15] One must recognize that part of Jesus' prophecy was directed to first-century Jewish disciples, but part of it to people living at a future

---

[13] Luke 2:7-15
[14] Matthew 2:9-11
[15] Luke 21:10, 11, 25-28

time. If one does not realize there are definite divisions and targeted groups for certain prophetic passages, then one can become confused. By keeping the verses in context and considering all scripture on a particular topic, one can correctly interpret it. We must therefore: *"Study to show ourselves approved unto God, workmen that need not to be ashamed, rightly **dividing** the word of truth."*[16]

---

[16] II Timothy 2:15

THE RAPTURE

What does the Bible tell us about the Rapture? It is an imminent event in which the dead and living believers in the Lord Jesus Christ are suddenly caught up to meet Him in the air. He then takes them to be with Him in Heaven. Though the term "Rapture" (per se) is not in the Bible, the event describing believers being "caught up" is--hence the designation "rapture." It is the bodily resurrection of believers when Jesus comes to rescue His Bride (the Church) from this world and to take them to Heaven before God's wrath is poured out upon the earth. The following scriptures describe this imminent evacuation of Christians from the earth:

*"But I would not have you to be ignorant, brethren, concerning them which are asleep, that ye sorrow not, even as others which have no hope. For if we believe that Jesus died and rose again, even so them also which sleep in Jesus will God bring with him. For this we say unto you by the word of the Lord, that we which are alive and remain unto the coming of the Lord shall not prevent them which are **asleep** [figurative description of believers who have died.[17]] For the Lord himself shall descend from heaven with a shout, with the voice of the archangel, and with the trump of God: and the dead in Christ shall rise first: Then we which are alive and remain shall be **CAUGHT UP** together with them in the clouds, to meet the Lord in the air: and so shall we ever be with the Lord. Wherefore comfort one another with these words."* (I Thessalonians 4:13-18)

In this passage, we see that this resurrection includes both living and dead believers in Christ at His coming. It is heralded by the sounding of the trumpet of God. We know that the spirits of dead believers are already in Heaven, for the Apostle Paul tells us, "to

---

[17] Acts 7:59-8:1

be absent from the body is to be present with the Lord."[18] When Jesus comes, He will bring the dead saints' disembodied spirits with Him. At the first trump, the dead saints' bodies are raised from the earth to be unified with their spirits. When the trump sounds again the believers' bodies are changed to immortality and are "caught up" to be with the Lord in the air. Jesus does not return to earth at this point, but takes His people back with Him to Heaven to enter into rest in their Heavenly bridal chambers. This resurrection takes place instantaneously:

"So also is the resurrection of the dead. It is sown in corruption; it is raised in incorruption: It is sown in dishonor; it is raised in glory: it is sown in weakness; it is raised in power: It is sown a natural body; it is raised a spiritual body. There is a natural body, and there is a spiritual body... Now this I say, brethren, that [natural] *flesh and blood cannot inherit the kingdom of God; neither does corruption inherit incorruption.*

*Behold, I show you a mystery; we shall not all sleep, but we shall all be changed—**in a moment, in the twinkling of an eye,** at the last trump: for the trumpet shall sound, and the dead shall be raised incorruptible, and we shall be changed. For this corruptible must put on incorruption, and this mortal must put on immortality. So when this corruptible shall have put on incorruption, and this mortal shall have put on immortality; then shall be brought to pass the saying that is written, Death is swallowed up in victory."[19]*

The mortal bodies that we now have will be changed into bodies that cannot die or corrupt. They will be perfect like Jesus' glorious, resurrected body.[20] Imagine… no pain, no sickness, no effects of aging… no limitations! After Jesus rose from the dead He appeared bodily to His disciples. He encouraged them to touch His hands[21] and feet where the nail prints were to see that He had a

---

[18] II Corinthians 5:8
[19] I Corinthians 15:42-54
[20] Philippians 3:21
[21] Luke 24:39

body of flesh and bones-- that He was not just a spirit. And yet His Glorious Body had the power to go through the walls of the locked house in which the disciples had gathered. Knowing that He would be returning to heaven soon, Jesus comforted His disciples with these words:

"Let not your heart be troubled: ye believe in God, believe also in me. In my Father's house are many mansions: if it were not so, I would have told you. I go to prepare a place for you. And if I go and prepare a place for you, <u>I will come again, and receive you unto myself; that where I am, there ye may be also.</u>"[22]

How beautiful this passage is! Jesus is very clearly referring to the traditional Jewish betrothal and wedding ceremony, as He describes the reunion of Himself with His Bride, the Church. The ancient Jewish wedding ceremony foreshadows the Rapture of the Church in many ways.

The first stage of the Jewish marriage was the entering into a legal contract by the bride and bridegroom. In the betrothal ceremony (*"kiddushin"*) they vow to commit to each other in marriage. "Kiddushin" means "sanctification" in Hebrew. The Bride of Christ is to be sanctified—that is, purified and separated from the world, and set apart exclusively for the Bridegroom.

Also, at the betrothal ceremony a "bride price" must be paid for the bride. The Heavenly Father spared no expense to purchase the Bride: ***"He that spared not His Own Son, but delivered Him up for us all, how shall He not with Him also freely give us all things?"*** (Romans 8:32) Such love the Father has bestowed upon us in giving heaven's best to purchase our souls! And such love that Christ has for His Church to be willing to lay down His life for us: ***"Unto Him that loved us, and washed us from our sins in His own blood."*** (Revelation 1:5) God considered us so valuable that He paid for us with His Own Blood!

---

[22] John 14:1-3

During the betrothal period, the bride prepared herself for the bride-groom and the bridegroom prepared a home for his bride. When the bridegroom had finished his preparations, he would return to the bride's home to bring her to the wedding. The time of his coming was a surprise. It was only when the bride heard the loud celebration of joyous shouts and rams' horns blowing by the approaching wedding party that she knew the bridegroom was coming.

He would then take her to the *"chupah"* (bride chamber) for the wedding ceremony and consummation of the marriage. This wedding feast typically lasted seven days. This foreshadows the seven years that the church will be hid in their heavenly bridal chambers while the inhabitants of the earth experience God's indignation:

"Your dead men shall live, together with My dead body shall they arise. Awake and sing, you that dwell in dust: for your dew is as the dew of herbs, and the earth shall cast out the dead. <u>Come, My people, and enter into your chambers</u>, and shut your doors behind you: hide yourselves as it were for a little moment, until the indignation be overpast. For, behold, the LORD comes out of His place to punish <u>the inhabitants of the earth</u> for their iniquity: the earth also shall disclose her blood, and shall no more cover her slain." (Isaiah 26:19-21)

THE BLESSED HOPE

What a terrible time those left on earth will experience! But, what a blessed hope that the Raptured believers have: being eternally united with the One who loved them enough to shed His own blood for them! The Bible states, *"In the presence of the Lord is the fullness of joy"*[23] and that *"eye has not seen, neither ears have heard, neither has entered into the heart of man the things that God has prepared for them that love Him."*[24] With great anticipation Jesus Christ, the Bridegroom, is waiting to catch away His Bride to be with Him in Heaven. It will be "joy unspeakable and full of glory" for true believers. We are admonished to look forward to this wonderful event, as it will motivate us to live Godly lives while we are here:

"For the grace of God that brings salvation hath appeared to all men, Teaching us that, denying ungodliness and worldly lusts, we should live soberly, righteously, and godly, in this present world; ***Looking for that blessed hope, and the glorious appearing of the great God and our Savior Jesus Christ."*** (Titus 2:12, 13)

The **appearing** of the Savior Jesus Christ is a "blessed hope" because He delivers believers from the coming wrath. Christians are to look for JESUS' appearing…NOT for God's wrath and judgment. What a great consolation to know that we will be with the Lord forever! Romans 5 states: *"But God commends his love toward us, in that, while we were yet sinners, Christ died for us. Much more then,* **being now justified by his blood, we shall be saved from wrath through him.** *For if, when we were enemies, we were reconciled to God by the death of his Son, much more, being*

---

[23] Psalm 16:11
[24] I Corinthians 2:9

reconciled, we shall be saved by his life." If God was willing to send Jesus to the Cross for us when we were His enemies, how much more is He willing to save those who have been reconciled to Him from the coming time of wrath and judgment? Our hope should be focused on Jesus coming to deliver us—not on God's wrath.

THE DAY OF THE LORD

The time of God's wrath and judgment is called the "Day of the Lord." Thessalonians 1:10 tells us that we are to *"wait for His Son from Heaven, Whom He raised from the dead, even Jesus, which delivered us FROM the wrath to come."* Here the Greek word is "apo", (meaning "from") NOT "ek" ("out of"). At the Rapture the Church is delivered FROM the coming wrath—not "out of." God's obedient children will not experience any of God's wrath, for He *"reserves His wrath for His enemies,"*[25] the *"children of disobedience."*[26] That is good news for those who have made Jesus the Lord of their lives: they will escape the coming wrath. But it is bad news for those who disobey. They will experience the most horrible time that mankind has ever faced on this earth. That time is called the "Great Tribulation" or the "Day of the Lord." These prophetic visions that follow are how God revealed this coming time of wrath to the ancient Hebrew prophets:

*"Woe unto you that desire the **day of the LORD**! To what end is it for you? The **day of the LORD is darkness**, and not light. As if a man did flee from a lion, and a bear met him; or went into the house, and leaned his hand on the wall, and a serpent bit him. Shall not the **day of the LORD be darkness**, and not light? Even very dark, and no brightness in it?"* (Amos 5:18-20)

This description reminds me of the dark—black—backdrop that I saw in my vision… with terrible danger and no place of safety.

*"Alas for the day! for **the day of the LORD is at hand**, and as a destruction from the Almighty shall it come. Is not the meat cut off before our eyes, yes, joy and gladness from the house of our God? The seed is rotten under their clods, the garners are laid*

---

[25] Nahum 1:2

[26] Colossians 3:6

desolate, the barns are broken down; for the corn is withered.
How do the beasts groan! the herds of cattle are perplexed,
because they have no pasture; yes, the flocks of sheep are made
desolate. O LORD, to You will I cry: for the fire hath devoured
the pastures of the wilderness, and the flame hath burned all the
trees of the field. The beasts of the field cry also unto You: for the
rivers of waters are dried up, and the fire hath devoured the
pastures of the wilderness." (Joel 1:15-20)

Our ecosystem is so dependent on the rain that God sends... We take His blessings so much for granted. The only difference between the United States and Somalia is a couple of years of extreme drought and no crops. During the Day of the Lord there will be great drought.

*"For the **day of the LORD** of hosts <u>shall be upon every one that</u>*
<u>is proud and lofty</u>, and upon every one that is lifted up; and he
shall be brought low" (Isaiah 2:12)

Pride is very prevalent in our society. Through pride we won't acknowledge our need for God, nor are we thankful for His blessings. It is a deception in perception to think that we do not need Him in our lives. During "the day of the Lord" God will allow those who reject His gift of love to experience a world without His love, His Light, or His peace:

*"Howl ye; for the **day of the LORD** is at hand; it shall come as a*
***destruction from the Almighty**. Therefore shall all hands be faint,*
and every man's heart shall melt: And they shall be afraid: pangs
and sorrows shall take hold of them; they shall be in pain as a
woman that travails: they shall be amazed one at another; their
faces shall be as flames.

*Behold, the **day of the LORD cometh, cruel both with wrath and***
fierce anger**, to lay the land desolate: and He shall **destroy the
***sinners** thereof out of it. For the stars of heaven and the*
constellations hereof shall not give their light: the sun shall be

*darkened in his going forth, and the moon shall not cause her light to shine. And I will **punish the world** for their evil, and the wicked for their iniquity; and I will cause the arrogancy of the proud to cease, and will lay low the haughtiness of the terrible. I will make a man more precious than fine gold; even a man than the golden wedge of Ophir. Therefore I will shake the heavens, and the earth shall remove out of her place, in the **wrath of the LORD** of hosts, and in the day of his fierce anger."* (Isaiah 13:6-11)

We are so used to seeing God as the loving, forgiving God that He is, that we sometimes forget that He is also a God of judgment. As the Apostle Paul tells us, "it is a fearful thing to fall into the Hands of the Living God..."[27]

The prophet Zephaniah also describes this time of God's wrath:

*"The great **day of the LORD** is near, it is near, and hastes greatly, even the voice of the **day of the LORD**: the mighty man shall cry there bitterly. That day is a **day of wrath, a day of trouble and distress, a day of wasteness and desolation, a day of darkness and gloominess, a day of clouds and thick darkness**, a day of the trumpet and alarm against the fenced cities, and against the high towers."*

*"And I will bring distress upon men, that they shall walk like blind men, **because they have sinned against the LORD: and their blood shall be poured out as dust**, and their flesh as the dung. Neither their silver nor their gold shall be able to deliver them in the **day of the LORD's wrath**; but **the whole land shall be devoured** by the fire of his jealousy: for he shall make even a speedy riddance of all them that dwell in the land."[28]*

---

[27] Hebrews 10:31
[28] Zephaniah 1:14

ESCAPING THE WRATH TO COME

Thank God that the Church will not have to experience God's wrath— it is reserved for His enemies—NOT for His beloved children! As I read these passages concerning the day of the Lord, I remember those images that I saw over 50 years ago... the darkness, the terror, the deprivation. I remember how people were so desperate for food and how those who had it would kill to defend their food supply.

What should one do if that time really IS upon us? (And I believe it is—and soon...) Should we hoard food and try to find a mountain cave in the Rockies or the Appalachians where we can hide out for seven years? NO! For one thing, the great destruction that will be unleashed upon the earth will be so widespread that there will not be any safe place to hide. At that time, there will be world-wide famine, drought, and likely biological, chemical, and nuclear weapons of mass destruction unleashed. Even the rich who have prepared fallout shelters in caves of mountains will experience God's wrath:

*"And the kings of the earth, and the great men, and the rich men, and the chief captains, and the mighty men, and every bondman, and every free man, **hid themselves in the dens and in the rocks of the mountains**; And said to the mountains and rocks, Fall on us, and hide us from the face of **Him that sits on the throne, and from the <u>wrath of the Lamb: For the great DAY OF HIS WRATH</u> is come; and who shall be able to stand?"*[29]

The safest place to be is in the Shadow of the Most High... that is, stay very close to God. He came to redeem people from their sin and will rescue those who become part of His family so that they do not have to experience the coming wrath.

---

[29] Revelation 6:15, 16

I would be remiss to go any further without inviting the reader to receive God's gift of salvation so that they too can be part of His family. Jesus offers forgiveness of sin to "whosoever will…" Not one of us *deserves* to go in the Rapture or escape God's judgment of eternal damnation in hell. Every one of us has sinned and fall far short of God's holy and righteousness standard.[30] The verdict for all of us is "guilty." The Bible states that "the wages of sin is death." God loved us so much that He allowed Jesus to pay the death penalty for our sins on the Cross.

If you will repent (turn from sin), ask Jesus to cleanse your sins with His Holy Blood, and commit to following Him as Lord of your life, you will be saved! You will become part of God's family. *"If you will confess with your mouth the Lord Jesus and believe in your heart that God has raised Him from the dead, you shall be saved."*[31] You will not only be saved from sin and eternal damnation, but also saved from *"the wrath to come."*

Here is Jesus' personal invitation to you: *"Behold I stand at the door and knock. If anyone opens the door, I will come in to them and sup with them and they with Me."*[32] This free gift of eternal life is yours for the asking. You simply receive it by faith. Once you have asked Jesus to be the Ruler of your life, you will have an inner peace and assurance. You will *know* that you are going to heaven.

There is nothing on earth…no amount of money or fame…that can compare with His peace. If you only knew how much God loves you, you would not hesitate a moment to make that decision. God gave me the vision as a warning of what **I would face** if I did not get saved. He also mandated that I warn others so that they will not have to experience that wrath.

---

[30] Romans 3:23, 6:23
[31] Romans 10:9, 10
[32] Revelation 3:20

GOD WILL DELIVER!

There are so many ways in which God is reaching out to mankind today to warn him to escape the impending judgment. He is giving supernatural visitations and visions (as I had); He is proving His great love and power by granting miraculous healings; and, He has given us the Biblical promises of deliverance from the wrath to come.

The following are some of my favorite scriptures regarding the promised deliverance from the *Day of the Lord's* wrath:

"But of the times and the seasons, brethren, ye have no need that I write unto you. For yourselves know perfectly that the **day of the Lord** *so comes as a thief in the night. For when* <u>they</u> [unsaved people of the world] *shall say, Peace and safety; then sudden destruction comes upon them, as travail upon a woman with child; and* <u>they</u> *shall not escape.* <u>But you, brethren</u> [Christians], *are not in darkness, that* **that day** *should* <u>overtake</u> [literally, come upon] *you as a thief. You are all the children of light, and the children of the day: we are not of the night, nor of darkness.*

Therefore, let us not sleep, as do others; but let us watch and be sober. For they that sleep sleep in the night; and that be drunken are drunken in the night. But let us, who are of the day, be sober, putting on the breastplate of faith and love; and for a helmet, the **hope of salvation** ["salvation" is "soteria" in the Greek, means "rescue, safety, deliverance, save".]

For <u>**GOD HAS NOT APPOINTED US TO WRATH**</u> *but to obtain* <u>salvation</u> [deliverance] *BY OUR LORD JESUS CHRIST, Who died for us, that, whether we wake or sleep,* [refers to believers alive or dead at the Rapture as described previously in chapter 4:14-18] *we should live together with Him. Therefore, comfort yourselves together, and edify one another."* (I Thessalonians 5:1-11)

Oh, my! The day of wrath (day of the Lord) will come suddenly and it will take those who are not ready for the Rapture by surprise. But, those who are saved have the wonderful comfort knowing that they will be delivered by Jesus from wrath!

Another wonderful promise of deliverance from God's wrath is prophesied by Jesus:

*"And take heed to yourselves, lest at any time your hearts be overcharged with surfeiting, and drunkenness, and cares of this life, and so **that day** come upon you unawares. For as a snare <u>shall it come on all them that dwell on the face of the whole earth</u>. **Therefore, watch and pray always that you may be accounted worthy to <u>ESCAPE ALL</u> <u>these things that shall come to pass, and to stand before the Son of man</u>.**"* (Luke 21:34-36)

If we watch and pray, staying spiritually alert, we will *escape all* of the day of the Lord's wrath. Thank God! In light of all of these wonderful promises, children of God should be looking forward to the Rapture! God has clearly promised that we are *"**not appointed for His wrath**,"* but will be delivered at the Rapture and *"escape all these things that shall come <u>upon the earth</u>,"* and *"stand before the Son of man."*

In spite of these very clear promises of deliverance from the wrath of God, some are confused about the timing of Rapture. They think that the Rapture of the Church is in the middle or at the end of the "Day of the Lord's wrath," and that they will have to endure at least a few years of His wrath. This is because they take some of the prophetic scriptures out of context.

Even in Paul's day there were some who misunderstood Paul's apostolic teachings concerning the Rapture. Some had taught that Christians would go through--or had *been* going through--the great tribulation. Paul was inspired to write another letter to the Church at Thessalonica to dispel that error and confusion. In the second letter to the Thessalonians, Paul explained that believers in Christ would not even be on the earth for the Day of the Lord and the subsequent revealing of the anti-Christ. Paul expounds this truth in 2 Thessalonians:

*"Now we beseech you, brothers, **by the coming of our Lord Jesus Christ, and by our gathering together unto Him** [the Rapture], that you be not soon shaken in mind, or be troubled, neither by spirit, nor by word, nor by letter as from us, as that the <u>day of Christ</u> is at hand. Let no man deceive you by any means: for that day* [the day of the Lord] *shall not come except there come a falling away** [departure] *first..."*

*The term that is translated in the King James Version as "falling away" is "apostasia" in the Greek. Greek scholars note in the Amplified Bible that in this passage "apostasia" can be interpreted as "**departure** of the Church." The root word for apostasia is "aphistemi" (Strong's Concordance # 868), which means "to remove, desert, depart, draw away, withdraw self." Though "apostasia" in some cases can infer "falling away" (as in "falling away" from the faith), in this case it refers to **the _departure_** (i.e., Rapture) *of the Church* before the day of the Lord's judgment. In keeping with the intent of Paul's message, which he explicitly states is to **encourage** the church with **_good hope_**, it is obvious that he is referring to the "blessed hope" of the Church when it departs at the Rapture.[33]

Paul begins the chapter stating what he is going to discuss: *"the coming of our Lord Jesus Christ, and our gathering together unto Him"* (i.e., the RAPTURE).[34]

The entire context of his message is to encourage believers that the departure of the Church (i.e., gathering together with Christ at the Rapture) occurs first, before the Day of the Lord's judgment commences. Only *then* (after the Church departs) can that wicked

---

[33] Titus 2:13
[34] II Thessalonians 2:1

one be revealed and God's judgments of wrath be poured out upon the world. The Rapture of the Church is *the departure* that occurs before the Day of the Lord's wrath.

Paul states *"**Don't let anyone deceive you... that day** [the day of God's wrath, the day of Christ]*[35] ***will not come except the apostasia** [departure of the Church] **occurs first**." Then* the man of sin (the anti-Christ) will be revealed. Here "apostasia" definitely refers to the departure of the Church. This is a singular event (**the** departure) that precedes the **day of the Lord**, at which time the antichrist is revealed. Paul had already assured the church that they were not appointed to experience God's wrath[36] that occurs during the Day of the Lord, but they would be delivered from "the wrath to come."[37]

A false teaching was upsetting the Thessalonian Church saying (contrary to Paul's first letter) that the Church was in the midst of the Day of the Lord's wrath. Some equated Caesar to the anti-Christ, and their suffering persecution as the "Great Tribulation." However, suffering persecution from sinners is not the same as experiencing the judgments of God's wrath. In this second letter Paul explains that though we may suffer for the kingdom of God *at the hands of sinners* (II Thes. 1:5-7), we will not be on earth to experience *God's wrath* during the 7-year tribulation.

*...departure first, and that man of sin be revealed, the son of perdition; who opposes and exalts himself above all that is called God, or that is worshipped; so that he as God sits in the temple of God, showing himself that he is God. Remember ye not, that, when I was yet with you, I told you these things? And now you know **what withholds** that he might be revealed in his time. For the mystery of iniquity does already work: only he* who now lets [restrains] will continue to restrain until he be **taken out of the way**.*

---

[35] Revelation 6:17
[36] I Thessalonians 5:9
[37] I Thessalonians 1:10

And then shall that wicked be revealed, whom the Lord shall consume with the Spirit of His mouth, and shall destroy with the brightness of His Coming:"

The only force on the earth that is hindering satan's power and that is going to depart (be *"taken out of the way"*) is the Church. Believers will **depart** when they are *"caught up to meet the Lord in the air"* at the Rapture. The Church (i.e., the Spirit of God within the Body of Christ) is the *"he that now restrains"* and holds back the antichrist spirit now. It is only *after* the church departs that *"then shall that wicked be revealed."*

God cannot leave His Church on the earth for the 7-year tribulation time. He promised that the Church was not appointed for His wrath, but to obtain His salvation and deliverance at the Rapture. Once He keeps His promise to rescue the Church from the earth, then the restraining force of the Holy Ghost in the believers will no longer be holding back the antichrist spirit from manifesting. Without the Church on the earth, the antichrist's demonic powers will be able to fully operate:

"Even him [anti-christ]*, whose coming is after the working of satan with all power and signs and lying wonders, and with all deceivableness of unrighteousness in them that perish; because they received not the love of the Truth, that they might be saved. And for this cause God shall send them strong delusion, that they should believe a lie: That they all might be damned who believed not the truth, but had pleasure in unrighteousness.*

But we are bound to give thanks always to God for you, brethren beloved of the Lord, because God has from the beginning chosen you to "salvation" ["soteria" rescue, safety, deliverance" at the Rapture-I Thes. 5:9, 10] through sanctification of the Spirit and belief of the truth: Whereunto He called you by our Gospel, to the obtaining of the glory of our Lord Jesus Christ. Therefore, brethren, stand fast, and hold the traditions which you have been taught, whether by word or our epistle. Now our Lord Jesus Christ Himself, and God, even our Father, which has loved us, and has given us everlasting __consolation and good hope__ through grace, comfort your hearts and establish you in every good word and work." (II Thessalonians 2:9-17)

Note that the doctrine of the pre-tribulation Rapture is always characterized as that which brings "good hope" and comfort to the saints. The entire purpose of Paul's letter to the Thessalonians was to assure them that they were not going to go through the time of God's wrath on earth. He wanted to encourage them that they would be gathered together to meet the Lord in the air and taken to heaven before the anti-Christ is revealed.

Paul was saying: *"__Don't let anyone deceive you into thinking that you are experiencing the Day of the Lord's wrath (the Great Tribulation), for that day won't come until the departure of the Church occurs first. Only THEN can the wicked antichrist be revealed. The Church is the force on earth hindering him from being revealed. Once the church departs at the Rapture, then the antichrist will manifest and deceive people who refused to love the knowledge of the truth to be saved. But we are thankful to God that you believers are chosen to be saved (rescued), so hold these truths fast. God has given you good hope!"__*

The true Church will not go through even one hour of God's wrath. Jesus promised that if we "watch and pray always" we can **escape _all_[38]** of the tribulation that is coming upon the earth. Confirming this, Jesus prophesied to the true Church (symbolized by the Church of Philadelphia) that they would **be delivered** from the time of *"temptation, which shall come upon **all the world,** to try __them that dwell upon the earth__."*[39] However, the worldly, backslidden Church (symbolized by the Church of Thyatira—one entrenched in spiritual wickedness) was warned **they** _would be_ cast into great tribulation--unless they repented!

---

[38] Luke 21:36
[39] Revelation 3:10

THOSE WHO ARE READY

Clearly, if one is watching and praying and looking for Jesus' return with a true heart of faith and love, then they will be delivered from ALL the great tribulation. However, if they are lukewarm, in sin, and are compromising with the world and false religion, then they should not expect to be caught up at the Rapture. They will not be delivered, but--according to Jesus in Revelation 2--they will be cast into Great Tribulation. In other words, some of the church will be raptured, but some will not. This is confirmed by Jesus' parable in Matthew 25:

*"Then shall the kingdom of heaven be likened unto ten **virgins**, which took their lamps, and went forth to meet the bridegroom. And **five of them were wise, and five were foolish.** They that were foolish took their lamps, and took no oil with them: But the wise took oil in their vessels with their lamps.*

While the bridegroom tarried, they all slumbered and slept. And at midnight there was a cry made, Behold, the bridegroom comes; you go out to meet him. Then all those virgins arose, and trimmed their lamps. And the foolish said unto the wise, Give us of your oil; for our lamps are gone out. But the wise answered, saying, Not so; lest there be not enough for us and you: but go you rather to them that sell, and buy for yourselves.

*And while they went to buy, the **Bridegroom** came; and they that were ready went in with him to the marriage: and the door was shut. Afterward came also the other virgins, saying, **Lord, Lord**, open to us. But he answered and said, truly I say unto you, I know you not. **Watch therefore, for ye know neither the day nor the hour wherein the Son of man comes.** "*

These "virgins" were symbolic of the Church: five were wise, and five were foolish. The wise prepared themselves and took oil in their lamps (symbolic of the Holy Ghost). The foolish had their initial "oil" (experience with God) but didn't bother to replenish it by staying in close communion with God. Other things entered into their hearts that took priority over their relationship with Jesus.

At the beginning of the Book of the Revelation Jesus is shown walking in the midst of the candlesticks (the Churches). In those 7 churches there "just happens to be" ten subgroups of believers— five wise, and five foolish:

All the members of the Church of Ephesus and the Church Laodicea needed to repent. There were "them" (some of) the Pergamos Church that held false doctrine that allowed for compromise with the world. The Church of Thyatira had some that committed spiritual adultery against Christ who would be cast into great tribulation. And, Sardis was a spiritually dead church where most did not maintain true faith in their lives. These are the "five foolish virgins" who will not go with the Bridegroom when He comes at the Rapture.

The wise virgins, however, will "*escape all these things and stand before the Son of Man.*" They are typified by the persecuted Church of Smyrna, those in Philadelphia who held fast love and spiritual power, and the remnant in Pergamos, Thyatira, and Sardis who walked righteously in faith and purity (in spite of the other, compromising church members). Notice that once the "door" (symbolic of entering Heaven)[40] is shut, the foolish virgins do not get a second chance. Those who do not take God's Word seriously but live careless lives will not be Raptured.

---

[40] Revelation 4:1

WHEN?

When can we expect this Blessed event? *No man knows the exact "day and hour,"* but when one sees the signs, they can *"**know it is near, right at the door.**"* (Matthew 24:33-36, 44) Hebrews 10:25 lets us know that we can *"**see the day approaching**,"* but still, we must never put an exact date on His coming. It is imminent, but only the Father knows the actual day.

The signs of His coming are so evident: The wars, rumors of war, massive earthquakes in various places, winds, hurricanes, tornadoes, terrorism, homosexuality, decadence of our society are all here now. They all point to Jesus' soon coming:

"For nation [literally, "ethnos"—ethnic group] *shall rise against nation* ["ethnos"], *and kingdom against kingdom: and there shall be famines, and pestilences, and earthquakes, in divers* ["throughout" i.e., wide-spread] *places. All these are the beginning of sorrows."*[41]

Notice the term "ethnos." Most of the conflicts throughout the world are different ethnic/religious groups fighting against each other within a country. The Muslims versus the Jews, the Hindis versus the Christians, the Sunnis versus the Shia Muslims... Also, the radicals against the established political ruling party as in Syria and Egypt are examples of "ethnos against ethnos."

Another sign, famine, sadly is becoming more and more widespread. The World Health Organization estimates that one-third of the world's population is starving. Every year 15 million children die of hunger. It doesn't always make the nightly news, but it is an ongoing global crisis.

---

[41] Matthew 24:7, 8

And then there are the earthquakes... In recent years, there has been the unprecedented upsurge in both frequency and intensity of devastating earthquakes: Bam, Iran- 43,000 dead... 8.8 earthquake hit central Chile, affecting about two million people; the Haiti earthquake had 316,000 people die, 300,000 injured, and 1,000,000 made homeless; the Sichuan Province China quake had over 80,000 casualties, 374,142 injured, and almost five million homeless; and Japan's 9.0 earthquake in 2011 was among the 5 strongest quakes ever recorded. In the past couple of decades, we have witnessed a 500% increase of earthquakes 7.0 and greater than any time in human history. Jesus said that these signs could be metaphorically likened unto labor pains: they would become more and more frequent and intense until the deliverance.

And then there are the "pestilences" (deadly diseases.) These are definitely on the rise. With the outbreaks of drug resistant malaria to the Ebola outbreaks, to AIDS... AID's is pandemic, killing almost 2 million annually.[42] Cancer affects 1 out of 3 females and 1 out of 2 males in the U.S. with over half a million deaths annually. Then there is the Corona Virus 19 pandemic and its mutant strains.

Jesus continues a few verses later to describe society: *"But of that day and hour knows no man, no, not the angels of heaven, but my Father only. But as the days of Noah were, so shall also the coming of the Son of man be. For as in the days that were before the flood they were eating and drinking, marrying and giving in marriage, until the day that Noah entered into the ark, And knew not until the flood came, and took them all away; so shall also the coming of the Son of man be. Then shall two be in the field; the one shall be taken, and the other left. Two women shall be grinding at the mill; the one shall be taken, and the other left. Watch therefore: for ye know not what hour your Lord does come."[43]*

---

[42] UNAIDS, WHO and UNICEF in November 2011
[43] Matthew 24:37-41

What were people doing in Noah's day? Eating, drinking… That seems to be America's favorite past time. As a result, America has an over 55% rate of obesity.

And then, there is the prediction about "marrying and giving in marriage…" The incessant cycle of marriage/divorce/re-marriage/divorce continues: 50% of 1st time marriages end in divorce; 75% remarry, and 60-80% of those marriages end in divorce. That is such a sad reality, and was never God's intent. The "marriage" sign also applies to the increase and acceptance of sinful and aberrant marriage practices, such as gay marriage.

Another aspect about society in the days of Noah's was that the people were violent.[44] Violent crime has increased over 300% in our generation.[45] (This does not even count the annual murder of 40+ million babies world-wide through abortion.)

Luke 21:10 also includes the curious phrase *"fearful sights."* In the Greek, this term ("phobetron") means "sights that evoke terror" or "instruments of terror." In recent years, we have seen a huge upsurge in terrorist attacks—probably due to the great publicity that terror groups receive by instant internet and satellite coverage of their horrific acts perpetrated against innocent men, women and children. Terrorism is now a favorite form of warfare.

Fear and stress are increasing to the point that the Bible states that it would be a major sign of the end: *"men's hearts failing them for fear."* This is certainly being fulfilled in that today heart failure is the number one killer in the United States.[46]

Further in the chapter Jesus tells us there will be *"signs in the sun, and in the moon, and in the stars; and upon the earth distress of*

---

[44] Genesis 6:2,5,11
[45] U.S. Census records, 2010
[46] CDC article 2010

nations, with perplexity; the sea and the waves roaring; Men's hearts failing them for fear, and for looking after those things which are coming on the earth: for the powers of heaven shall be shaken."[47]

How many lunar and solar eclipses have we seen lately? Some see the unusual phenomenon of the tetrad of "blood moons" as a fulfillment of "signs in the moon." And, with the current political and economic chaos, there is definitely "distress of nations with perplexity" (the leaders not knowing *how* to solve the global problems.)

The sea and the waves "roaring" is a sign fulfilled with the marked increased hurricanes and "tsunamis" (including "super tsunamis"—the proportions of which were almost unheard of until recent years.) The five most destructive U.S. hurricanes in terms of dollars all occurred within this past decade. Tornados ("whirlwinds") also have increased markedly in America. Sadly, this is a latter-day sign that there is much immorality in the religious leadership of our country. According to Jeremiah both tornadoes and drought are signs of Divine judgment of sin in the pulpit:

"The land is full of <u>adulterers</u>; for because of swearing the land mourns; the pleasant places of the <u>wilderness are dried up</u>, and their course is evil, and their force is not right. For both prophet and priest are profane... Behold, a <u>whirlwind</u> of the LORD is gone forth in fury, even a grievous whirlwind: it shall fall grievously upon the head of the wicked...

The anger of the LORD shall not return, until he has executed, and till he has performed the thoughts of his heart: <u>in the latter days</u> you shall consider it perfectly... I have not sent these prophets, yet they ran: I have not spoken to them, yet they prophesied. But if they had stood in my counsel, and had caused my people to hear my words, then they should have turned them from their evil way, and

---

[47] Luke 21:25, 26

from the evil of their doings.[48]

Here God clearly states that because of false prophets (religious leaders who prophesy for gain and are immoral), the land will suffer from drought and whirlwinds (tornadoes.) How many "prophets" do we hear today that brazenly proclaim "thus says the Lord" only to tickle the ears and take advantage of the unsuspecting, undiscerning Church? Scripture warns us of these false prophets:

"For when they speak great swelling words of vanity, they allure through the lusts of the flesh, through much wantonness, those that were clean escaped from them who live in error."[49]

False prophets are popular prophets. They "prophesy" of fame, prosperity and the glory, but never address the sin that is in the camp. And, they are not accountable! When their "prophecy" does not come to pass, no one calls them on it! The Bible says we are to "test all things." If what they *said* was from God does not come to pass, then they were lying. The "after the fact" excuse for their false prophecy is commonly "it was a conditional Word" or they simply don't mention it again in hopes that people forget they lied.

Some of these "prophets" and "apostles" hold to false doctrines... even denying Jesus' Divinity or that He came in the flesh. This is antichrist doctrine. One such popular church leader, Rick Joyner, wrote in his popular book, There Were Two Trees in the Garden, that Jesus' body after the resurrection was only spiritual... that He does not have a glorified, physical body now.[50] That false teaching is of the *anti-Christ* spirit![51]

Other signs of false prophets include embracing organizations that teach doctrines contrary to the Word of God. Some popular religious

---

[48] Jeremiah 23
[49] II Peter 2:18
[50] Rick Joyner's book, "There Were Two Trees in the Garden" p. 59
[51] II John 7-10

leaders promote Roman Catholicism (in the interest of "unity," of course) and even join or promote anti-God organizations such as the Knights of Malta and Freemasonry. Much of Roman Catholic doctrine is not Biblical. Multiplied millions of faithful Catholics have lost their souls as they sincerely do penance, pray to Mary, make confession to a priest, take communion, but are never told "you must be born again."[52]

Remember, the antichrist and the false prophet come looking like a "lamb" but their words are from the devil![53] Look at the big push for "ecumenicalism" with the Pope at the forefront. The stage is being set for people to receive the antichrist, who will come in on the coattail of "unity": one world church, one world government, one world economy, one world military, etc. All this under the flattering guise of "peace" and "reconciliation."

The biggest threat to the Truth is not the obvious anti-God Islamists, but the deception from within the "Church," that has carried many sincere, unwitting souls astray. Just because someone may have great miracles in their "ministry" does not mean that they are of God. Jesus said MANY would declare to Him all of the miracles that they did in His name, and yet Jesus will say to them "depart from Me you workers of iniquity."[54]

Signs *and wonders do not necessarily validate a ministry* as being from God! There is much New Age occult practice being received into the church today. Just because it glitters doesn't mean it is really gold! The Word of God teaches that *there are legitimate signs and wonders* available to every believer for the purpose of effectively evangelizing the world.[55] However, the devil can also manifest miracles, as Jannes and Jambres did in the days of Moses.[56] God actually warns us that there will be prophets that show signs and wonders and then advocate going after other gods (i.e., following

---

[52]John 3:3-7
[53] Revelation 13:11
[54] Matthew 7:18-22
[55] Mark 16:15
[56] Exodus 7:22

doctrines that are contrary to God's Word.) God commands us not to listen to them! Deuteronomy 13 states:

*"If there arise among you a prophet, or a dreamer of dreams, **and gives thee a sign or a wonder, And the sign or the wonder come to pass**, whereof he spoke unto thee, saying, Let us go after other gods, which thou hast not known, and let us serve them; Thou shalt not hearken unto the words of that prophet, or that dreamer of dreams: for the LORD your God proves you, to know whether ye love the LORD your God with all your heart and with all your soul."*

False prophets are certainly on the increase with their insidious antichrist and new age doctrine. **Watch out for those who promote "spiritual" experiences but belittle the Word of God.** Paul warned the Corinthians that even though they had many manifestations and spiritual gifts, that they could receive **another spirit** from false apostles.[57] A spiritual sign or experience that does not put the focus on and exalt Jesus Christ and His crucifixion and resurrection is not from God. The Spirit of Truth glorifies Jesus.[58] The spirit of error exalts men, angels, ministries, and manifestations.

Test all things by the Word, the Spirit, and by the fruit. In II Timothy 3:1-5 the Apostle Paul explicitly describes the state of today's society:

*"This know also, that in the last days perilous times shall come. For **men shall be lovers of their own selves, covetous, boasters, proud, blasphemers, disobedient to parents, unthankful, unholy, without natural affection, trucebreakers, false accusers, incontinent, fierce, despisers of those that are good, traitors, heady, highminded, lovers of pleasures more than lovers of God; having a form of godliness, but denying the power thereof: from such turn away.** For of this sort are they which creep into houses, and lead captive silly women laden with sins, led away with divers lusts, ever learning, and never able to come to the knowledge of the truth. Now as*

---

[57] II Corinthians 11:3, 4
[58] John 16:13, 14

Jannes and Jambres withstood Moses, so do these also resist the truth: men of corrupt minds, reprobate concerning the faith. But they shall proceed no further: for their folly shall be manifest unto all men, as theirs also was."

The pervasive trend in our society is the show of *disrespect* that children have for their parents and all *authority*. This fulfills the "disobedient to parents" prediction. So prevalent is the defiance in children toward authority, now that the mental health community have coined a new "disorder" called ODD (Oppositional Defiance Disorder). In other words, children defy and oppose anything the parent or authority figure tells them.

The fulfillment of being *"without natural affection"* is evidenced when a mother drives her toddlers into a lake to drown them so she can date; or to bag up a suffocated daughter and bury her so "mom" can have fun partying with her friends.

Unnatural affection is also that spirit that causes one to reject the God-ordained relationship of a male and female and pursue the <u>same sex</u>, as it was in the days of Lot in Sodom and Gomorrah. God made it clear that if He did not spare that generation for their immoral affront to God's righteous standards, that He will not spare ours either. God loves the sinner, but that sin is an abomination to Him. Sadly, the immorality is not limited to "the world" or those who do not know Christ. It is among "Christians"—even preachers—who "have a form of godliness" but deny the power thereof.

#1 PROPHETIC SIGN

Based on the social and moral trends, the unprecedented natural disasters, the global economic and political upheavals, we can certainly conclude that Bible prophecy is being fulfilled. It all points to the end of the age. The most obvious sign, however, and one that defies any subjective interpretation, is the fact that the *nation of Israel* has been reestablished. As the Bible predicted, Israel is a sovereign nation planted back in the ancient land that God promised to them. This is the number one prophetic sign: the **Jewish State of Israel**. God prophesied that in the last days He would bring the Jewish people back into their own land:

*"But you, **O mountains of Israel, shall shoot forth your branches, and yield your fruit to my people of Israel**; for they are at hand to come. For, behold, I am for you, and I will turn unto you, and you shall be tilled and sown: And I will multiply men upon you, **all the house of Israel**, even all of it: and the cities shall be inhabited, and the wastes shall be built: And I will multiply upon you man and beast; and they shall increase and bring fruit: and I will settle you after your old estates, and will do better unto you than at your beginnings: and you shall know that I am the LORD."*[59]

*"... **in the latter years** you shalt come into the land that is brought back from the sword, **and is gathered out of many people, against the mountains of Israel**, which have been always waste: but it is brought forth out of the nations, and they shall dwell safely all of them."*[60]

We see Ezekiel references the people of Israel being brought back from the sword in the latter years. That certainly has come to pass. After the horrors of the Holocaust in World War II, the Jewish people were finally given back their homeland in Israel in 1948.

---

[59] Ezekiel 36:8-11
[60] Ezekiel 38:8

Psalm 102 gives a prophetic and eerie foreshadowing of the atrocities that the Jewish people endured. Parts of it are reminiscent of Ann Frank's diary that describes *living on the house top*. Her Jewish family had to hide in the attic chambers from the Nazi's until they were discovered and taken to the concentration camps. There are also allusions to the Jews' starvation and the notorious ovens of Hitler:

*"Hear my prayer, O LORD, and let my cry come unto thee. Hide not thy face from me in the day when I am in trouble; incline thine ear unto me: in the day when I call answer me speedily. For **my days are consumed like smoke, and my <u>bones are burned as an hearth</u>**. My heart is smitten, and withered like grass; so that I forget to eat my bread. By reason of the voice of my groaning my **bones cleave to my skin**. I am like a pelican of the wilderness: I am like an owl of the desert. I watch, and am as a sparrow **alone upon the house top**. **Mine enemies reproach me all the day; and they that are mad against me are sworn against me**...*

*But thou, O LORD, shalt endure forever; and thy remembrance unto all generations. **Thou shalt arise, and have mercy upon Zion: for the time to favor her, yea, the <u>set time</u>, is come.** For thy servants take pleasure in her stones, and favor the dust thereof. So the heathen shall fear the name of the LORD, and all the kings of the earth thy glory.*

***<u>When the LORD shall build up Zion, He shall appear in his glory</u>. He will regard the prayer of the destitute, and not despise their prayer. This shall be written for <u>the generation to come</u>:** and the people which shall be created shall praise the LORD. For he hath looked down from the height of his sanctuary; from heaven did the LORD behold the earth; **To hear the <u>groaning of the prisoner</u>; to loose those that are <u>appointed to death</u>; To declare the name of the LORD in Zion, and his praise in Jerusalem."*

The horror that the Jews endured is unthinkable. But, thank God, the LORD did favor Israel at the "set time," May 14, 1948! He kept His covenant with the Jewish people and brought them back from the sword to their own land... the mountains of Israel. And now

Zion (Israel as a whole and Jerusalem particularly) is "built up." The Jewish people have turned the desert waste places into fruitful places and the "desert is blooming like a rose!"[61]   Israel is the breadbasket for that part of the world, producing some of the finest fruits and vegetables through their high tech agricultural land development. Prophetically speaking, the "*generation to come*" is **May 14, 1948. Zion is now "*built up.*"** The rest of that prophetic scripture will also be fulfilled. Therefore, we can expect the Lord to "*appear in his glory*" very soon!

Jesus gives us additional insight concerning the timing of His coming. In the midst of His prophecy concerning the last days with all of the signs referenced before, Jesus says the end time generation should "behold the **fig tree**." According to scripture, the fig tree represents the nation of Israel and the Jewish people. Confirming this is the passage in the Book of Joel in which the prophet references the "fig tree" as He describes Israel's impending judgment:

*"He hath laid my vine waste, and barked **my fig tree:** he hath made it clean bare, and cast it away..."[62]*

The prophet Hosea also equates Israel to a fig tree:

*"I found **Israel** like grapes in the wilderness; I saw **your fathers as the first ripe in the fig tree...**"[63]*

Jeremiah also refers to the Jewish people as "figs":

*"One basket had very good figs, even like the figs that are first ripe... Like these **good figs**, so will I acknowledge **them that are carried away captive of Judah**, whom I have sent out of this place into the land of the Chaldeans for their good. For I will set mine eyes upon them for good, and **I will bring them again to this land: and I will build them, and not pull them down; and I will plant them, and not pluck them up.** And I will give them an heart to know me,*

---

[61] Isaiah 35:1
[62] Joel 1:7
[63] Hosea 9:10

that I am the Lord: and they shall be my people, and I will be their God..."[64]

What Jesus was really saying in His fig tree parable was: "Watch Israel." That will be the sign that you are to look for in order to know that you are in the generation that will see "all these things fulfilled." Before May 14, 1948 it was not possible to "behold the fig tree." But now she is established: the fig tree has taken root in her own land; she has "shot forth her branches"[65] and is flourishing. We are the generation that will see all of Jesus' prophecies of the end fulfilled. As previously quoted, Psalm 102 states that "when the Lord builds up Zion [which He has] *He shall appear in glory."* What a wonderful promise! Our generation that has seen Israel re-established will see the coming of Lord for His Church at the Rapture!

---

[64] Jeremiah 24:5-7
[65] Ezekiel 36:8

THE FIG TREE GENERATION

When will this take place? We must know how to define a Bible "generation" to understand that. When Moses was told to number the people of His generation, he was told to count those who were adults. According to Numbers 14 and Hebrews 3:10, God said that the **generation** (those who were adults, twenty years and older) that would not trust Him, could not enter the promise land; and that **that "generation" grieved Him.** Moses' "generation" only included the adults. We can conclude that, based on Biblical interpretation ("comparing spiritual things with spiritual" and scripture with scripture), those twenty years old and over when Israel was established are **"this generation"** that will not pass away until **"all these things are** fulfilled." The very youngest of the 1948 fig tree generation is now 93 years old [in 2021.] Jesus said that all of His prophecy (which includes the Rapture, the subsequent seven-year tribulation, and His second coming) would be fulfilled **before this generation** passes away.

If the Rapture happened tonight, then add 7 years. The very youngest of this generation would be 100 years old when the prophecies are all fulfilled. Given that the average Biblical life span is 70 years (or 80 if one is healthy)[66] we don't have long! All the signs are here, so it is definitely time to *"look up for your redemption draws near!"*[67]

---

[66] Psalm 90:10
[67] Luke 21:28

THE SIGNS ARE HERE

So, let's sum it all up: The signs of Jesus' coming are all around. At any moment, believers can expect Jesus' appearance in the clouds. At that time, He will take the faithful to Heaven before God's wrath is poured out upon the earth. Scripture is clear on this. Still, some professing Christians remain confused. They think they will go through God's wrath because they read in the Bible about "the saints," and "the elect" who must endure to the end of that horrible time of judgment on earth.

What they do not recognize is that God has more than one group to whom He gives the designation "elect" or "saints." After the Church is Raptured, then God's focus is no longer on the Church, but on the nation of Israel. There are still seven prophetic years that must be fulfilled with that nation. The coming Day of the Lord (great tribulation time) is also called the "time of **Jacob's** [Israel's] **trouble.**"[68] That is when God brings about national salvation and deliverance for the Jewish people of Israel.

During the tribulation, one group designated as "elect" is the 144,000 Jewish "servants of our God." They receive their Messiah Jesus after the Rapture, and—along with the two prophets—are instrumental in preaching Yeshua (Jesus) to the nation of Israel.[69] The Apostle Paul tells us that now (during the Church Age), *"blindness in part has happened unto Israel until the time of the fullness of the Gentiles* (i.e., Gentiles saved during the age of grace) *be come in..."*[70]

The Church Age concludes at the Rapture. Then, the focus on earth

---

[68] Jeremiah 30:7
[69] Revelation 7:3-8
[70] Romans 11:25

is no longer the Church (which is in Heaven), but the nation of Israel and the Jewish people. During the time of "Jacob's trouble" the Jewish nation's spiritual eyes will be opened and they will receive their Messiah, Yeshua, and be saved. They are then the "elect." Also, some Gentiles will get saved at that time—though it will be a very horrible time, as they will not be spared God's judgments or persecution from the anti-Christ. They are also considered "elect" and "saints." They must endure to the end without taking the mark of the beast, and must be willing to be beheaded for their testimony of Christ.[71]

---

[71] Revelation 20:4

RIGHTLY DIVIDE

Based on scripture, which cannot be broken, negated, or contradicted, the true Church is not appointed to God's wrath (the Day of the Lord). Christians will not go through *any* of the seven-year tribulation. The reason some become confused is that they read Jesus' prophecies, but do not recognize that He is prophesying to different groups of people at different prophetic times. Part of His message is directed to the tribulation saints (not to the Church under grace.)

Making it a little more complicated is the fact that some Biblical prophecies have a 2-fold fulfillment...a partial, near (immediate) fulfillment, and a complete, far (futuristic) fulfillment. There is an example of this in the Book of Daniel. Daniel prophesies about the "abomination of desolation" which was fulfilled *in part* by Antiochus Epiphanes in 168 BC[72], but will not be completely fulfilled until the anti-Christ defiles the Temple during the tribulation (almost 2,200 years later.)[73] Both are referred to as "the abomination that makes desolate."

Also, the prophet Isaiah prophesied of a son being born before judgment came. It was partially fulfilled in Isaiah's wife bearing a son (Isaiah chapter 8), but the prophecy was not completely fulfilled until seven hundred years later when, at Christ's birth, "Immanuel" was born.[74]

The purpose of a partial, immediate fulfillment was to validate the prophet's words as being truth to his generation so that his words

---

[72] Daniel 8
[73] Mark 13:14
[74] Isaiah 7:14

would be preserved as valid prophecy. Christ's prophecies frequently have a 2-fold fulfillment. For instance, in Luke 21 He stated that the Temple would be destroyed (which occurred in 70 AD) and, when armies would surround Jerusalem, the inhabitants should flee. This was fulfilled partially in the first century, but the complete fulfillment (which includes the anti-Christ setting himself up in the Temple of God) will not be accomplished until the middle of the tribulation period.[75]

In order to properly understand prophecy, one must realize that Jesus directs His prophecies to different groups at different times. It was clear to His 1st century disciples that Jesus targeted different groups when He taught and prophesied. Peter asked Him, *"Lord, are You speaking this parable unto us* [exclusively], *or even to all?"*[76]

Matthew 24 is a classic prophecy chapter in which Jesus addresses 4 different groups at three different times in history, spanning almost 2,000 years. (Hence, the need to "rightly divide" the Word, so that one does not take a passage out of context and apply it to a particular group to whom it was not directed.) Not everything that Jesus prophesied is directed to all people or to every dispensation. The general principles do apply to everyone (e.g., faithfulness to the Lord and watchfulness is necessary for all believers); but His *exact directives* apply only to a specific group.

Jesus addresses the Jewish believers of the first century, who would see the Temple destroyed. Then He addresses the Church, who would see the signs of His coming. And then, He addresses the tribulation saints—those Jewish and Gentile believers who receive Jesus as Messiah after the seven years of judgment commence.

"And Jesus went out, and departed from the temple: and his disciples came to him for to show him the buildings of the temple. And Jesus said unto them, See ye not all these things? Truly I say

---

[75] Matthew 24:15, II Thessalonians 2:4
[76] Luke 12:41

unto you, there shall not be left here one stone upon another, that shall not be thrown down. [Jesus refers here to the destruction of the Temple in Jerusalem by the Romans in 70 A.D.] *And as he sat upon the Mount of Olives, the disciples came unto him privately, saying, Tell us, when shall **these things be**? And what shall be the* **sign of Your coming**, *and of the* **end of the world**?"

Here three different times are inquired about by His disciples: The Temple's destruction, that occurred in 70 A.D.; the signs of Jesus' coming, referred to as the "beginning of sorrows" (which we currently see today); and the "end of the world"—the time when Jesus returns at the end of the seven-year tribulation to judge the nations and to begin His 1,000-year reign.

"And Jesus answered and said unto them, Take heed that no man deceive you. For many shall come in my name, saying, I am **Christ; and shall deceive many.**[77] *And ye shall hear of wars and rumors of wars: see that ye be not troubled: for all these things must come to pass, but the end is not yet.* [Note: This is the first time Jesus warns of false Christ's and/or prophets. Here it is directed to the Church] *for nation shall rise against nation, and kingdom against kingdom: and there shall be famines, and pestilences, and earthquakes, in different places. All these are the* **beginning of sorrows**. [The "sorrows" refer to birth pangs, which increase in frequency & intensity as birth approaches. So, natural disasters, violence and turmoil will continue to increase as Jesus' return approaches.] Then is the watch word "**then**" (time change):

*"**Then** shall they deliver you up to be afflicted, and shall kill you: and ye shall be hated of all nations for my name's sake. And then shall many be offended, and shall betray one another, and shall hate one another. And many* **false prophets** *shall rise, and shall deceive many. And because iniquity shall abound, the love of many shall wax cold. But he that shall endure unto the end, the same shall be saved. And this gospel of the kingdom shall be preached in all the world for a witness unto all nations; and then shall the end come."*

---

[77] False prophets of our time: Jim Jones, Father Divine, David Koresh, Sun Yung Moon

After the "beginning of sorrows" section directed to believers before the Rapture, Jesus then directs His prophecy to the tribulation "elect" (those who receive Jesus as Messiah after the Rapture.) During the time of Jacob's Trouble there will be not only the antichrist and the false prophet, but many false prophets in Israel trying to deceive the Jewish people. Some will actually try to impersonate Jesus by having their hands pierced.[78]

Jesus warns that during this time family members will betray one another to death, as Micah 7 warns. The prophet states that during the time of "God's indignation" (i.e., "Jacob's Trouble") there would be *no righteous* people left on the earth. "The righteous have *'abad'*" ("wandered away" "become lost"—i.e., they are gone.) This implies that the rapture has occurred, leaving only unbelievers on earth when the time of God's wrath commences.[79] Isaiah 57 confirms this by stating "the righteous are *taken away from the evil to come,"* and will enter into their heavenly chambers of peace.[80]

Then those Jews (who, *after* the Rapture, have their spiritual eyes opened and receive Christ) are warned to *guard* what they say—even to family members.[81] Family members will betray their own flesh and blood and turn them over to be killed by the antichrist. In the middle of the tribulation, all are commanded to worship the antichrist and take his mark. Those that do not comply will be beheaded.[82]

Then Jesus specifically addresses the *Jewish* elect in Judaea in the midst of seven years when the antichrist invades Jerusalem:

---

[78] Zechariah 13:3-6
[79] Micah 7:1-9
[80] Isaiah 57:1, 2; Isaiah 26:19-21
[81] Micah 7:5,6
[82] Revelation 20:4

*"When **you therefore shall see the abomination of desolation,**
spoken of by Daniel the prophet, stand in the **holy place,** (whoso
reads, let him understand.) Then let them which be **in Judaea flee
into the mountains**: Let him which is on the housetop not come
down to take anything out of his house: Neither let him which is in
the field return back to take his clothes. And woe unto them that
are with child, and to them that give suck in those days! But pray
ye that your flight be not in the winter, **neither on the Sabbath day:**
For then shall be **great tribulation,** such as was not since the
beginning of the world to this time, no, nor ever shall be. And except
those days should be shortened, there should no flesh be saved: but
for the elect's sake those days shall be shortened."*

With the references to the abomination of desolation in
the Holy Place (Temple Mount), Judaea, and the Sabbath day
regulations, it is obvious this prophetic warning from Jesus is
directed to the **Jewish elect** during the time of "Jacob's Trouble"
–not to the present-day Church.

In addition to the Jewish elect, Jesus also warns the rest of the "elect"
tribulation saints who "keep the commandments of God and have the
testimony of Jesus Christ."[83] They must "endure to the end" without
succumbing to the anti-Christ. They also are warned of false
prophets:

*"Then if any man shall say unto you, Lo, here is Christ, or there;
believe it not. For there shall arise **false Christs, and false prophets**,
and shall show great signs and wonders; insomuch that, if it
were possible, they shall deceive the very elect. Behold, I have
told you before. Wherefore if they shall say unto you, Behold, he
is in the desert; go not forth: behold, he is in the secret chambers;
believe it not. For as the lightning cometh out of the east, and
shines even unto the west; so shall also the coming of the Son of
man be. For wheresoever the carcass is, there will the eagles be
gathered together."*

---

[83] Revelation 12:17

Notice Jesus *__again__* warns of "false Christ's and false prophets" for the third time. He is not being redundant. He is warning 3 different groups at three different times in this discourse: The Church, the tribulation saints (who must endure to the end of the 7 years), and the Jews who witness the antichrist invasion in the middle of the tribulation.

Among those who receive Messiah during Jacob's trouble are the 144,000 "sealed" Jewish evangelists,[84] who have the distinct blessing of being raptured in the midst of the seven years. The tribulation saints also receive Jesus, but they are not taken out of the judgments on the earth. Rather, they must "endure to the end" of the seven-year tribulation wrath. It is the *tribulation saints* who have to experience the Great Tribulation (the latter half of the seven years of wrath)—*not the Church* or the 144,000 elect, Jewish evangelists.

When talking specifically to the **Jewish people in Jerusalem,** Jesus refers to the **"abomination that makes desolate"** in the *__Jewish__* **Temple,** to the *__Jewish__* **"Sabbath day's journey,"** and to fleeing **Jerusalem** to the safety of the mountains across the Jordan River in "Sela."[85] He directs this to the Jews who are on earth during "*Jacob's* (Israel's) trouble" — NOT to the Christians who are already Raptured! The context of the prophecy defines the group to which Jesus is prophesying:

*"Immediately **after the tribulation of those days** shall the sun be darkened, and the moon shall not give her light, and the stars shall fall from heaven, and the powers of the heavens shall be shaken: And then shall appear the sign of the Son of man in heaven: and then shall **all the tribes** of the earth mourn, and they shall see the Son of man coming in the clouds of heaven with power and great glory. And he shall send his angels with a great sound of a trumpet, and they shall gather together **his elect** from the four winds, from one end of heaven to the other."*

---

[84] Revelation 7:3-8
[85] Isaiah 16:1

This passage is directed to the tribulation saints who must endure through the latter half of the seven-year tribulation without denying Christ. At the end of the tribulation there will be very obvious signs heralding Jesus' return to the earth (unlike the Rapture that is in secret seven years before). At the end of the tribulation (when Jesus returns to earth **_with_ the Church**) He "gathers together" (resurrects) the "elect" who endured to the end. They will join Jesus' great processional as He returns with His saints to reign in Jerusalem. Jesus concludes by informing us of the generation that would see all of these things fulfilled:

*"Now learn a parable of the fig tree; When his branch is yet tender, and puts forth leaves, ye know that summer is near: So likewise, when you shall see all these things, **know that it is near**, even at the doors. Truly I say to you, **this generation** shall not pass, till all these things be fulfilled. Heaven and earth shall pass away, but my words shall not pass away. But of that **day and hour knows no man**, no, not the angels of heaven, but my Father only."*

We know that "the generation" that sees Israel established (May 14, 1948) will see the Lord's appearance.[86] Jesus continues by warning that the people of the last generation will be so engaged with their normal lives, that they will be oblivious to His coming. Like Noah's day, some will be saved (Raptured), but most will be lost.

"But as the days of Noah were, so shall also the coming of the Son of man be. For as in the days that were before the flood they were eating and drinking, marrying and giving in marriage, until the day that Noah entered into the ark, And knew not until the flood came, and took them all away; so shall also the coming of the Son of man be. Then shall two be in the field; the one shall be taken, and the other left. Two women shall be grinding at the mill; the one shall be taken, and the other left."[87]

---

[86] Psalm 102
[87] Matthew 24:37-41

During the tribulation, a total of half the world's population is killed. If one considers there are almost 8 billion people alive today, then 4 billion will die. At the beginning one-fourth (2 billion) are destroyed (Rev. 6:8). Later in Rev. 9:18 another 1/3 of the remaining six billion are killed (2 billion more.) This equates to one of every two being "taken" in death. It's notable too, that only one out of every two Christians is taken in the Rapture. Remember the ten subgroups of the seven Churches in Revelation 2 and 3? Five were wise and went with the Bridegroom, but the foolish five were left behind. It's the same ratio: 1 taken, 1 left behind.

PLEASE NOTE: Those who have heard the Gospel but are not ready for Jesus' coming ARE NOT promised another chance! Paul states in II Thessalonians that those who have heard the Truth--but don't love God enough to obey it--will be deceived by the anti-Christ and damned to hell. Don't have a "Left Behind" mentality of "if I miss the Rapture, I'll get saved later." The spirit of deception, especially during the last half of the tribulation, will be so strong that even the very elect could be deceived. Remember, Jesus warns us that heaven's door will not be opened to those who were not ready for His coming (symbolized by the five foolish virgins).[88] He warns the Church to be constantly ready for His coming will be when you least expect it.

"Watch therefore: for ye know not what hour your Lord doth come. But know this, that if the goodman of the house had known in what watch the thief would come, he would have watched, and would not have suffered his house to be broken up. Therefore **be ye also ready: for in such an hour as ye think not the Son of man comes."**[89]

Christ's commands us to **watch and to be ready.** Again, that implies that He can come at any time: His coming is imminent. He promised

---

[88] Matthew 25
[89] Luke 12:40

that if we watch and pray always, we can **"escape all** these things!" Jesus promised to deliver the true Church (represented by the Church of Philadelphia) from the time of **"temptation"**:

*"These things says He that is holy, He that is true, He that has the key of David, He that opens and no man shuts; and shuts and no man opens; I know your works: behold, **I have set before you an open door**, and no man can shut it: for you have a little strength, and have kept My word, and have not denied My Name. Behold, I will make them of the synagogue of satan, which say they are Jews, and are not, but do lie; behold, I will make them to come and worship before your feet, and to know that I have loved you. Because you have kept the word of My patience, **I also will keep you from the hour of temptation, which shall come upon all the world, to try then that dwell upon the earth.** "Behold, I come quickly: hold fast which you have, that no man take your crown.* "[90]*

Jesus promised to rescue His people from the time of great trial that will come upon all the world (the Great Tribulation.) Though Christians may suffer at the hands of sinners while on earth—as represented by the persecuted Church of Smyrna in Revelation 2— it is not the same as experiencing God's wrath during the "Day of the Lord." Persecution is not **God's** wrath upon the Church, but tests that the devil causes Christians to suffer. Notice also that Jesus tells the true Church, **"I have set before you an open door."** This "open door" symbolizes entering into heaven, as Rev. 4:1 and II Peter 1:11 indicate. Because they had been faithful, Jesus promises that they will escape the hour of temptation on the earth by entering the open door to heaven. They escape God's wrath, that those who are left behind on the earth must endure.

Must Differentiate!

Please realize that there is a difference between the Rapture and the Second Coming of Christ. They occur at different times. The

---

[90] Revelation 3:7-11

Rapture (the blessed hope of the Church) occurs <u>before</u> the 7-year tribulation. The Second Coming of Christ is at the <u>end</u> of the tribulation (when Jesus returns <u>with His Church</u> to reign on earth.) The Rapture could occur any time, and it will be a <u>surprise</u> (as "**a thief in the night**").

Because Jesus' coming at the Rapture is imminent (can occur at any moment), believers are admonished to always anticipate His coming, and to maintain a state of readiness: "***be ye also ready: for in such an hour as you think not the Son of Man comes.***"[91]

After the Church is Raptured, God's focus changes to the Jewish people. It is important to note that during the entire seven-year tribulation (Revelation chapter 6 through chapter 19) **the Church** <u>is only depicted</u> **in Heaven.** At the conclusion of Jacob's seven years of trouble, the Church returns <u>with Jesus</u> to deliver Israel and t o destroy the anti-Christ. (See Revelation 19:11-14 and Zechariah 14.) When Christ returns at the end of the tribulation, it is *not a surprise* (as is the case with the Rapture), but is heralded by many prophetic signs:

"<u>*Immediately*</u> *after the tribulation of those days shall the sun be darkened, and the moon shall not give her light, and the stars shall fall from heaven, and the powers of the heavens shall be shaken: And then shall appear the sign of the Son of Man in heaven: and then shall* <u>***all the tribes of the earth mourn, and they shall see the Son of Man coming in the clouds***</u> *of heaven with power and great glory.*" (Matthew 24:29, 30)

Here, the exact timing of Christ's Second Coming is told to us: "*immediately after the tribulation of those days.*" At the beginning of the tribulation the anti-Christ signs a seven-year covenant that will allow the Jews to offer sacrifice on Temple Mount. (The anti-

---

[91] Matthew 24:42

Christ breaks that covenant when he invades Jerusalem after 3 ½ years.) At the end of the seven years, Messiah Jesus returns to rescue the Jewish nation. The timing of the second coming is known based on the signing of the covenant (treaty.)

When Jesus returns to earth at the second coming, the whole world will see Him: "ALL THE TRIBES OF THE EARTH" shall see the Son of Man. However, at the Rapture, Jesus only appears "**to them that look for Him**" (Hebrews 9:28). At the Rapture Jesus comes FOR His Church. At the Second Coming, however, the Church ("saints") returns **WITH Him,** clothed in fine linen,[92] to execute judgment on the nations at Armageddon:

*"Then shall the Lord go forth, and fight against those nations ... And His feet shall stand in that day upon the Mount of Olives, which is before Jerusalem...and the Lord My God shall come, and **ALL the saints with Him**."[93]*

The timing of the Second Coming *is known* (after the seven-year tribulation.) The timing of the pre-tribulation Rapture *is not known*, for Jesus can come at any time--"as a thief in the night."

No One Knows...

It is important to realize that *no one knows* the "day or the hour" of Jesus' return for the Church: *"**the Son of Man comes at an hour that you think not**.*" Some note that Jesus fulfilled Jewish feasts with His death and burial (at Passover and Unleavened Bread), with His resurrection (First Fruits), and at Pentecost (by sending the Holy Spirit at the birth of the Church.) Many assume that the Feast of Trumpets will be fulfilled by the Church at the Rapture, and so set the date for the Rapture to coincide with that Jewish Feast day (e.g., September 9th, 2018.) They expect Jesus to come on that feast day, and go so far as to predict it. Remember the book, "88 Reasons Why the Rapture Will Be in 1988"? It is always wrong to set a date,

---

[92] Revelation 19:7, 8, 11-14
[93] Jude 14, 15; Zechariah 14

or limit the Rapture to a certain day or year.

One must remember that Jesus said His coming is when you *do not expect Him*. He can come any time! The Church (the Body of Christ) is called *"First Fruits"* unto God in Romans 8:23 and James 1:18. The gathering of the Church at the Rapture is not necessarily the main "harvest" that will be fulfilled at the Feast of Trumpets. There are multiple resurrections after the Church's Rapture that could fulfill that "ingathering" feast. Those who said the Rapture would be on the Feast of Trumpets in September 2015, for instance, were inadvertently and erroneously declaring they *knew* that Jesus was not coming *prior to* or *after* that Feast. Setting a date for Jesus' imminent coming for the Church is not scriptural.

However, we can know the exact timing of the *Second Coming*. Simply add seven years from the day that the Church is Raptured, and then Jesus will return to reign on the earth. BUT the timing of the Rapture of the Church will be a surprise… "as a thief in the night"—unexpected and imminent.

BOOK OF REVELATION OVERVIEW

Understanding that Jesus comes for the Church before the seven year tribulation, for the 144,000 in the middle of the seven years, and for the Jews and tribulation saints when He returns at the end of the seven years, makes the Book of the Revelation much less confusing. It can be understood in a chronological and generally literal manner. God does everything "decently and in order" and He is not the author of confusion. When He states, "after these things" in the Book of the Revelation, it means just that: events follow in sequential order. Jesus' give us an exact outline of the Book of the Revelation: *"Write what you have seen, the things that are, and the things that shall be hereafter."[94]* That which John the Revelator "**had seen**" was the glorified Christ:

"And I turned to see the voice that spoke with me. And being turned I saw seven golden candlesticks; And in the midst of the seven candlesticks One like unto the Son of Man. And when I saw Him, I fell at His feet as dead. And He laid His right Hand upon me, saying unto me, Fear not; I am the first and the last; I am He that liveth, and was dead; and behold, I am alive for evermore, Amen; and have the keys of hell and death."[95]

Then Jesus says to write "the things **which are**." The things present in John's time were the seven Churches of Asia. They represent the Church Age from the first century until Jesus Raptures the Church. **Revelation chapters 2 & 3** describe Jesus' prophecies to the seven Churches. These Churches are in chronological order. The last Church (Laodicea) describes the Christian Church of today—lukewarm and without the zeal of the early Church. However, these 7 Churches are also characteristic of

---

[94] Revelation 1:9
[95] Revelation 1:12-16

Christians of every age (some lukewarm; some doctrinally off; some persecuted unto death; some faithful and overcoming.) He writes to the true Church:

"Behold, I have set before you an <u>open door</u>, and no man can shut it. Because you have kept the word of My patience, I also will <u>KEEP YOU FROM the hour of temptation</u>, which shall come upon <u>all the world, to try THEM THAT DWELL UPON THE EARTH</u>."

The true Church will not be on the earth for that time of testing. They go through the open door to Heaven:

*"<u>**After this**</u> I looked, and, behold, a **door was opened in heaven**: and the first, voice which I heard was as it were of **a trumpet** talking with me; which said, "**Come up hither**, and I will show you things which must be <u>**hereafter**</u>." And immediately I was in the spirit; and, behold, a throne was set in heaven, and One sat on the throne."* (Revelation 4:1, 2)

The Church enters Heaven by the "open door" and so escapes the *"hour of temptation which shall come upon all the world..."* The open door and phrase "come up hither" refers to being Raptured. The fact that the Church is already in Heaven *before* the judgment seals of Revelation 6 are loosed, is confirmed in Revelation 4:4

*"And round about the throne were four and twenty seats. And upon the seats I saw **four and twenty elders** sitting, clothed in white raiment; and they had on their heads **crowns of gold**."*

Paul states in II Timothy 4:8 that the Church will receive their crowns *"**at that day**"* (when Jesus appears for the Church at the Rapture). Crowns are given to the Body of Christ at the Rapture:

*"Henceforth there is laid up for me a **crown of righteousness**, which the Lord, the righteous Judge, shall give me at <u>**that day**</u>: and not to me only, but unto <u>all them</u> also that love **His appearing**."*

I Peter 5:4 also states that the "crowns" are given to believers when Jesus appears:

"And <u>when the chief Shepherd shall appear, you shall receive a crown</u> of glory that fades not away."

The fact that the elders in heaven already have crowns on their heads in Revelation 4, indicates Jesus had *already appeared* (R a p t u r e d t h e C h u r c h), and had given believers their respective crowns. The Rapture occurs *before* the Revelation 6 seals of wrath are opened at the beginning of the 7-year tribulation.

Then He said to write "the things which shall be **hereafter**." The "hereafter" (after the Church's Rapture) is the **Day of the Lord.** During the entire seven years (Revelation chapters 6-19) the Church is only seen in Heaven.

Beginning with **chapter 6** the seals of God's wrath are loosed upon the earth. At this time, the anti-Christ begins to conquer people politically and militarily, as represented by the white horse. As an impersonator of the true Christ, the anti-Christ arrives on the scene, riding a white horse (as Jesus will do when He returns at the end of the seven years). The other horses represent war, famine, and death. By these ¼ of the world's population dies (approximately two billion people). Those who receive Christ after the Rapture (the tribulation saints) have to endure these judgments of God (Rev. 6:8-11). Many tribulation saints die at this time. Their souls are seen clothed in white robes under the altar of God in Heaven.

Chapter 7 depicts these martyrs before the throne: *"These are they which came out of great tribulation."* Their bodies are not yet resurrected. They simply died from the judgments in the earth, and their souls are in Heaven awaiting their resurrection.

At the beginning of the tribulation (the first 42-weeks of the seven years) there will be two witnesses that God sends to earth. They will testify to the world about Jesus the Messiah, especially to the Jewish people in Israel. Some who did not get the opportunity to hear the Gospel before will hear it then. God has mercy in the midst of judgment, and many will be saved during the tribulation.

Some think the wrath of God is not poured out until the second half of the tribulation. That is not so. Even at the beginning of the seven-year time of trouble, it is a time of God's judgment and wrath. The earth's inhabitants will to try to "hide from the face of Him that sits on the throne and from ***the wrath of the Lamb***." (Rev. 6:17) Before the middle of the tribulation, ½ of the world's population is already destroyed. The reason the second half is sometimes called "great tribulation" is because it is then that the Jews in Israel will suffer greatly (when the anti-Christ invades Jerusalem).

In **Revelation 7:3-8** the 144,000 elect Jews— "servants of our God"— are sealed. They **alone** are sealed as God's ***bond servants*** since the Church is in heaven. They will hear the message of the two witnesses sent from Heaven and receive Messiah Jesus. At this time, God has shifted His focus back to the nation of Israel to complete their last seven prophetic years. These elect, 144,000 sealed Jews will testify of Jesus to help open the eyes of their Jewish brethren. They are **virgin, Jewish males** from each of the twelve tribes of Israel. These are the only "servants of the Lord" on earth at that time. They preach to the rest of the nation of Israel (along with Elijah) so that the **"hearts of the fathers"** turn **"to the children"** (Malachi 4:6.) The "elect" here is NOT the Church. These are literal Jews: 12,000 from each of the 12 tribes of Israel.

As we progress through the Book of the Revelation, there are more judgments. God's wrath is released at the blowing of seven trumpets. **Revelation 8:1-13** describes God's judgment in the form of hail and fire, mingled with blood is cast to the earth. This causes 1/3 of the earth's grass and trees to be burned up. One third of the sea turns to blood, destroying sea life and ships. One third of lakes and rivers are contaminated by a possible nuclear source (star? satellite?) causing many to die. It is interesting that there was a military nuclear-powered satellite sent up in the early 1980's named "Wormwood." Additionally, 1/3 of the sun, moon and stars are darkened.

Revelation 9 describes strange, tormenting locusts with a scorpion-type sting (vs. 1-12.) Verses 15-19 describe a massive army of 200,000,000 (China and the kings of the east) being unleashed to destroy 1/3 part of mankind by "fire, smoke and brimstone." This seems to indicate a massive nuclear attack. Those not killed by these plagues still refuse to repent of their idolatry, murders, sorceries (drug use, witchcraft), immorality, and thefts.

In the next chapter, Revelation 10, we see a reference to the 144,000 Jews' Rapture. It is called it the "mystery of God":

"But in the days of the voice of the seventh angel [half of the way through the seven-year tribulation] *when he shall begin to sound, the mystery of God should be finished, as He declared..."*

This "seventh angel" sounds in chapter 11 and then the offspring of the woman, Israel, is caught up to God. This is the 144,000 elects' mid-tribulation Rapture.

Revelation 11 describes the ministry of the two witnesses. These two prophets prophesy for the first 1,260 days of the tribulation. Elijah is one of the prophets, as Malachi 4:5 states. The other is likely Enoch (who, along with Elijah, never had a physical death). They have power to shut up heaven so it will not rain in the days of their prophecies, and power to turn waters to blood and to cause plagues of all types. The anti-Christ will kill them halfway through the seven years. After the anti-Christ kills these two prophets, God raises them back to life t h r e e days later in the sight of the whole world (satellite coverage?) Then the seventh angel sounds.

Chapter 12 describes the "mystery of God," when He Raptures the sealed 144,000 Jews. This mystery occurs *"when the 7th angel begins to sound"* (right after the two witnesses are resurrected). Verses 1 and 2 depict a pregnant woman with twelve stars on her head. This is an Old Testament type of the nation of Israel:

"Before she travailed, she brought forth; before her pain came, she was delivered of a man child. Who has heard such a thing? Who has seen such things? Shall the earth be made to bring forth in one day? Or shall a nation be born at once? For as soon as Zion travailed, she brought forth her children." (Isaiah 66:7, 8)

This "pregnant woman" does not refer to the Church. The Church is the **Virgin**[96] Bride who does not complete her marriage feast to the Lamb until Rev. 19:7. This woman with child is the nation of Israel. The twelve stars represent the twelve tribes of Israel.[97]

The satan-inspired European Union-based "beast" (the anti-Christ with the help of ten "kings") then invades Israel. (Though the EU has more than ten nations under its jurisdiction, there will be ten leaders who are incorporated to *"reign AS kings"* and support the antichrist's agenda for world domination. It is interesting that the Western European Union in Brussels had only ten full voting members in its defense committee.[98] Perhaps the antichrist will incorporate a similar military "committee" when he gives those ten leaders power to reign with him, and so fulfill the prophecy of the "ten crowns" of the beast.) In any case, the antichrist invades Jerusalem at the 3 1/2-year point of the tribulation.[99]

Daniel 11:45 states that when the anti-Christ invades Israel and "plants his tabernacle" in the holy mountain, then shall Michael (the archangel) deliver Daniel's people. The timing for the 144,000 Jews to be "delivered" (raptured) is for a *"time, times, and a half*

---

[96] II Corinthians 11:2; Matthew 25:1
[97] Genesis 37:9, 10
[98] http://www.eeas.europa.eu/csdp/about-csdp/weu/index_en.htm
[99] Daniel 7:24, 25 & Daniel 9:27

a time" corresponding to Revelation 12:5, when the offspring of the woman Israel is *"caught up unto God and to His throne."* This "man child" refers to the sealed Jews who will reign in Jesus' Name and authority over the *"nations with a rod of iron."* The mystery is that God's sealed remnant Jews will be delivered out of the midst of the tribulation. No other converts during the tribulation period have the distinction of being "sealed" (protecting them from judgments) and the designation as being "firstfruits." (The Church that is raptured before the seven years starts is also designated as "firstfruits unto God.") After the 144,000 Jews finish their purpose of evangelizing, they will be raptured. Then, the "woman" Israel flees into the wilderness mountains for safety during the anti-Christ invasion of Jerusalem.[100] Isaiah states:

"from Sela to the wilderness ...hide the outcasts; betray not him that wanders, Let Mine outcasts [Jews who flee Israel] dwell with you, Moab; be thou a covert to them from the face of the spoiler" (anti-Christ.)

Some have reported that Bibles, food, and water have been store in the cliff city, Petra, anticipating the Jews who will eventually seek refuge there. This could be the *"place prepared of God, that they should feed her there a thousand two hundred and three-score days"* (the last 3 1/2 years). The woman is given wings of a great eagle (maybe a U.S. aircraft?) that she might fly into the wilderness to be nourished *"for a time, and times, and half a time, from the face of the serpent"* (**anti-Christ forces**).[101] The Anti-Christ military forces then take over Temple Mount, and the anti-Christ sets himself up in the Temple. At that time, he seeks to persecute the rest of the tribulation saints who *"keep the commandments of God, and have the testimony of Jesus Christ."* (vs. 17) These are the tribulation saints who must "endure to the end" to be saved.

Revelation 13 describes the anti-Christ as gaining world-wide

---

[100] Zechariah 14:1-5, Matthew 24:15-28
[101] Revelation 12:6, 14

dominion with its military forces. He deceives the world into worshipping him and blasphemes God. Then, intense persecution against the saints who refuse to worship him begins. He gains complete control over the world's economy to try to force everyone to receive an identification mark in their right hand or in their forehead to buy or sell. Microchip implant identification is already being used to help identify some patients' pertinent medical information quickly in case of a medical emergency. It is a small step to mandate microchip implants to buy or sell, especially after the economies of the world have crashed. Already European countries are becoming "cashless," making the "**mark of the Beast**" computerized microchip/microdot technology a necessity to buy or sell. It is interesting that the world's main banking terminal is in Brussels, Belgium (the headquarters of the European Union). This banking terminal is called the Brussels's Electronic Accounting Surveillance Terminal, known as the "B.E.A.S.T." (A coincidence? Probably not...) The number of the Beast (antichrist) is the number of a man: six hundred threescore and six.

<u>Revelation 14</u> begins by describing the 144,000 raptured, elect Jews as in heaven before God's throne. They are those who "**were redeemed from the earth.**" Those who think that the Church is Raptured in the middle of the tribulation do so because of several passages that describe a mid-tribulation Rapture. But the mid-tribulation rapture is NOT for the Church. It is only for the 144,000 sealed, elect, Jewish evangelists ("Daniel's people"):

*"And at that time shall Michael stand up, the great prince which stands for the children of **thy people** [the Jews]: and there shall be a time of trouble, such as never was since there was a nation even to that same time: and at that time **thy people shall be delivered**, every one that shall be found written in the book... And I heard the man clothed in linen, which was upon the waters of the river, when he held up his right hand and his left hand unto heaven, and swore by him that lives forever that it shall be for a **time, times, and an half;** and when he shall have accomplished to scatter*

*t he   power   of   the   holy   people,   all   these   things   shall   be
finished.*"[102]

The fact that this Rapture of the 144,000 elect Jews has occurred
in middle of the tribulation is confirmed in Revelation 14 (the
middle point of "Jacob's Trouble") where John writes:

"And I looked, and, lo, a Lamb stood on the [Heavenly] mount
*Zion, and with him **an hundred forty and four thousand,** having his
Father's name written in their foreheads. And I heard a voice
from heaven, as the voice of many waters, and as the voice of a great
thunder: and I heard the voice of harpers harping with their harps:
And they sung as it were a new song **before the throne,** and before
the four beasts, and the elders: and no man could learn that song
but **the hundred and forty and four thousand, which were
redeemed from the earth**. These are they which were not defiled
with women; for they are virgins. These are they which follow the
Lamb whithersoever he goes. These were redeemed from among
men, being the firstfruits unto God and to the Lamb."*

Verse 6 states that an angel ("angelos" / messenger) flies in the midst
of heaven and preaches the gospel to all that dwell on the earth.
There have been satellites launched into outer space actually named
"Angel 1" and "Angel 2." Since angels have never been used in
God's economy to preach the Gospel, it is possible that a satellite
"messenger" is alluded to here. A warning is given to any who might
receive the mark of the beast and worship him, that, in so doing, they
will incur the wrath of God and face eternal torment in hell. Angels
are seen reaping the earth. Some see this "reaping" as the main harvest
(resurrection) of tribulation saints. It follows the "firstfruits" (the
144,000 Jews' Rapture, as depicted in Revelation 12). This seems to
be verified in chapter 15 where the saints are described as going
through the "fire" (tribulation) and yet came out victorious over the
antichrist.

Revelation 15 describes angels in heaven having the last 7 plagues

---

[102] Daniel 12:1, 7

to pour out on the earth. In heaven, a group of tribulation saints are seen worshipping God: *"And I saw as it were a sea of glass mingled with fire: and them that had gotten the <u>victory</u> over the beast, and over his image, and over his mark, and over the number of his name, stand on the sea of glass, having the harps of God. And they sing..."* The "sea of glass" saints refused the mark of the beast and were killed for their testimony of Jesus. They endured persecution and martyrdom.

Chapter 16 describes God's judgment in the form of various plagues. These include a grievous sore on those who had the mark. Interestingly it was reported in the 80's that the lithium type batteries used with microchip technology could result in leakage that would cause severe ulcerations in the skin. Perhaps this is the source of the "grievance sores." At that time the sea, rivers and all water sources become blood; the sun scorches men with great heat; and darkness covers the anti-Christ's dominion. A great earthquake also levels the cities of the earth, and great hailstones weighing 100 pounds each fall upon men. We cannot even fathom the effects of such devastation! In the midst of this great judgment the inhabitants of the earth blaspheme God. Instead of repenting of their sin, they blame and curse God.

Then, the Euphrates River dries up. This allows for the Kings of the East (China and its allies) to make their way to Armageddon. **Revelation 17** describes a "great whore that sits upon many waters." This is a false religious system that has influence over many peoples[103] (waters). She sits on the beast with seven heads and ten horns. This symbolizes the anti-Christ power base of the revived Roman Empire, commonly known as the European Union. Interestingly, the basis for the EU was the "Treaty of Rome." The seven heads are the seven mountains of the city of Rome (commonly called the "City of Seven Hills"[104]).

The woman situated in Rome is not Christ's Bride, but a harlot religious system that persecutes the true church. The "whore" was responsible for the death of true believers ("prophets and apostles"). Historically, the city of Rome has been a source of persecution of true Christians throughout the ages. From the Caesars to the Roman

---

[103] Revelation 17:15
[104] Encyclopedia Britannica

Catholic Crusades and the Inquisition, this seat of false religion and pagan idolatry mirrors the religion of Babylon in that it promotes the worship of the "Queen of Heaven" (the Virgin Mary).[105] The woman is seen *"drunken with the blood of the saints and with the blood of the martyrs." This false "church" works with the anti-Christ to promote worship of the beast by appearing as a lamb (that is, trying to appear that it represents Christ the Lamb), but is actually speaking for the devil, the dragon.*

Eventually the control that this false religion has over the peoples of the earth will cause the anti-Christ forces to resent the church's influence. They will *"hate the whore and shall make her desolate and burn her with fire... the woman* [whore] *which you saw is that great city which reigns over the kings of the earth."*

Chapter 18 describes Babylon as fallen. In this case, "Mystery Babylon"[106] is definitely referring to the Roman Catholic church that sits on the Seven Hills of Rome. It is a religious system that historically has **spilled the blood of the martyrs and the apostles**. This fulfillment of Mystery Babylon's judgment occurs during the tribulation, and refers to the false religious system seated in Rome. The admonition is to *"Come out of her, My people ...that you receive not of her plagues...for her sins have reached unto heaven, and God has remembered* [indicating a long period of existence] *her iniquities."* Does this mean that God hates Catholics? ABSOLUTELY NOT! But He hates that religious system that deceives them into thinking they must go through another mediator other than Jesus Christ to get to God. Jesus said, "I am the way, the truth, and the life: no one comes to the Father **BUT BY ME.**"[107] The Bible clearly teaches "there is only ONE mediator (the Lord Jesus Christ) between God and man"[108]— NOT the Pope, a priest, the Virgin Mary, or a saint! The great wealth of the Vatican and its destruction are then described. God commands heaven to rejoice at

---

[105] Jeremiah 44
[106] See Revelation 18 notes on additional interpretations of "Mystery Babylon"
[107] John 14:6
[108] I Timothy 2:5

the judgment of that great city, because God has avenged the blood of the apostles and prophets and saints on her. Rome is the city and seat of false religion responsible for shedding the blood of saints and apostles. It is "**Mystery Babylon**."

Revelation 19 begins by praise to God for judging the great whore. Then, in contrast, the true Bride of Christ (the Church in heaven) makes herself ready for the marriage supper of the Lamb (vss.7-9). She is clothed in fine linen, clean and white, symbolizing the righteousness of the saints. Jesus prepares to return with His army of believers to battle the anti-Christ and his forces who are gathered at the valley of Armageddon (vss.11-19.) Notice, the Church returns WITH Jesus from Heaven. He is *"The Word of God"* and *"King of Kings and Lord of Lords."* He casts the beast and the false prophet alive into the lake of fire.[109] The rest of the anti-Christ forces are killed by the sword which proceeds out of Christ's mouth at Armageddon. Then the vultures devour them.

Chapter 20 depicts the devil being bound for a thousand years. The return of Jesus with His saints at the end of the tribulation begins the thousand-year (Millennial) reign of Christ with His Church. Christ and His Church will *"rule the nations with a rod of iron."[110]* At this time the bodies of the tribulation martyrs who had to "endure to the end" are resurrected and they will also reign with Christ. This is called the "first resurrection," a *category* reserved for the righteous. That category includes Jesus' resurrection[111], the Old Testament saints' resurrection,[112] the Church's pre-tribulation Rapture,[113] the two witnesses' resurrection,[114] the 144,000[115] mid-tribulation rapture, and then the final resurrection of the righteous at Jesus' return at the second

---

[109] Revelation 19:20
[110] Revelation 2:26, 27
[111] Matthew 28:6
[112] Matthew 27:52
[113] I Thessalonians 4:14-18
[114] Revelation 11:11
[115] Revelation 12:5

coming.[116] Jesus states there are two main categories of resurrection: the resurrection of life (for the righteous) and the resurrection of damnation (for those who have done evil.)[117] The tribulation martyrs are part of the "first resurrection" category and are resurrected at the end of the seven-year tribulation.

After Jesus' thousand-year reign, God will resurrect the rest of the dead and they will be judged at the Great White Throne Judgment. Anyone not written in the book of life will be cast into hell. At this time the devil will be cast into the lake of fire and brimstone to be tormented day and night for ever and ever.

Chapter 21 describes the new heaven and new earth where God will dwell with His people: *"And God shall wipe away all tears from their eyes; and there shall be no more death, neither sorrow, nor crying, neither shall there be any more pain: for the former things are passed away... He that overcomes shall inherit all things; and I will be his God, and he shall be My son.*

But the fearful, and unbelieving, and the abominable, and murderers, and whoremongers, and sorcerers, and idolaters, and all liars, shall have their part in the lake which burns with fire and brimstone: which is the second death."

Then the New Jerusalem is described: a city foursquare with jasper walls made of pure gold. There is no temple in it for *"the Lord God Almighty and the Lamb are the temple of it."* Only the saved shall be there, those whose names *"are written in the Lamb's book of life."*

In **Revelation 22** Jesus says:

"Behold, I come quickly; and My reward is with Me to give every man according as his work shall be." John then prophesies saying:

"For I testify unto every man that hears the words of the prophecy

---

[116] Luke 14:14
[117] John 5:29

of this book, If any man shall add unto these things, God shall add unto him the plagues that are written in this book: And if any man shall take away from the words of the book of this prophecy, God shall take away his part out of the book of life, and out of the holy city, and from the things which are writ- ten in this book. He which testifies these things says, 'Surely I come quickly.' Amen."

God has given us the complete revelation of the future. He warns us to flee from the wrath to come and extends the Blessed Hope to "whosoever will." That hope is the imminent coming of Jesus Christ to take His Bride, the Church, to Heaven with Him.

By the grace of God, the Church will not experience any of God's wrath, for she is "caught up" to meet her Bridegroom in the air. Jesus bids His people that are living in this last, prophetic "fig tree" generation to join Him:

*"The fig tree puts forth her green figs... **Arise, my love, my fair one, and come away.**"*[118]

Even so, come Lord Jesus! Maranatha!

---

[118] Song of Solomon 2:13

QUESTIONS RE: THE RAPTURE & RESURRECTION

1.) WHY IS UNDERSTANDING THE RESURRECTION IMPORTANT?

The most important fact in Christianity is that Jesus Christ was resurrected from the dead. It was that fact that caused His followers to be willing to lay down their lives to attest to His resurrection. They could not deny it. Over 500 of Jesus' disciples saw Him at one time after He was raised from the dead. They touched Him... they ate with Him. The first century disciples' greeting was "He is risen," to which they would reply, "He is risen indeed." This truth of Jesus' resurrection from the dead catapulted them to zealously evangelize the world and turn their world right-side up. Today that same reality gives believers in Christ Jesus the power to turn from sin and follow the one Who abides within. It is not religion, but a personal encounter with the Risen Savior.

Why is the resurrection of Jesus Christ from the dead so important to the Christian faith? Because without the resurrection, we are not forgiven of our sin! We <u>must believe</u> that God did the impossible by raising His Son from the dead. I Corinthians 15 states:

*"Now if **Christ be preached that he rose from the dead, how say some among you that there is no resurrection of the dead? But if there be no resurrection of the dead, then is Christ not risen: And if Christ be not risen, then is our preaching vain, and your faith is also vain.** Yea, and we are found false witnesses of God; because we have testified of God that he raised up Christ: whom he raised not up, if so be that the dead rise not. For if the dead rise not, then is not Christ raised: **<u>And if Christ be not raised, your faith is vain; ye are yet in your sins.</u>** Then they also which are fallen asleep in Christ are perished."*

God could not justify any of us based on our sinless lives (for all of us have sinned-Romans 3:23.) Instead, He chose to justify us by faith. True faith believes what God says— even if it seems impossible. Romans 10:9 states: *"That if thou shalt confess with thy mouth the Lord Jesus, and shalt **believe in thine heart that God hath raised him from the dead**, thou shalt be saved."* Faith in Jesus' resurrection from the dead saves us from sin.

We must also recognize the truth that Christ was raised **bodily** from the dead. Liberal theologians, who deny the inerrancy of Scripture, deny the physical resurrection of Christ. They believe that He was only raised spiritually, for that doesn't require the miraculous power of God and is much easier to rationalize. It is true that Jesus' resurrected, glorified body had supernatural attributes; however, it was still His physical body. After His resurrection, the disciples examined the nail scars in His hands and feet, and held Him by His feet. Jesus ate broiled fish and honeycomb in front of them:

"And as they thus spoke, Jesus Himself stood in the midst of them, and said unto them, Peace be unto you. But they were terrified and affrighted, and supposed that they had seen a spirit. And He said unto them, Why are you troubled? and why do thoughts arise in your hearts? ***Behold My hands and My feet, that it is I Myself: handle me, and see; for <u>a spirit hath not flesh and bones</u>, as you see Me have.***

And when He had thus spoken, He showed them His hands and His feet. And while they yet believed not for joy, and wondered, He said unto them, Have ye here any meat? And they gave Him an piece of a broiled fish, and of an honeycomb. And He took it, and did eat before them.

And He said unto them, These are the words which I spoke unto you, while I was yet with you, that all things must be fulfilled, which were written in the law of Moses, and in the prophets, and in the psalms, concerning Me. Then opened He their understanding, that they might understand the scriptures, And said unto them, Thus it is written, and thus it behooved **Christ to suffer, and to rise from the dead the third day.** *"* (Luke 24:39-43)

But the greatest proof is Jesus' own declaration in John 2:19-22:

"Jesus answered and said unto them, Destroy this temple, and in three days I will raise it up. *Then said the Jews, Forty and six years was this temple in building, and wilt thou rear it up in three days?* **But He spoke of the temple of His body.** *When therefore* **He was risen from the dead,** *His disciples remembered that He had said this unto them; and they believed the scripture, and the word which Jesus had said."*

The Apostle John emphasizes the physical human nature of Christ Jesus:

"That which was from the beginning, which we have heard, which we have seen with our eyes, which we **have looked upon, and our hands have handled, of the Word of life;[2]** *(For the life was manifested, and we have seen it, and bear witness, and show unto you that eternal life, which was with the Father, and was manifested unto us;)[3] That which we have seen and heard declare we unto you, that ye also may have fellowship with us: and truly our fellowship is with the Father, and with his Son Jesus Christ."* (I John 1:1-3)

John states here that they "handled" the Word of Life. In other words, Jesus was FLESH. The disciples touched Him after His resurrection. He left in His glorified, visible, physical body. In Acts chapter 1 the angels told the disciples who saw Jesus ascend that He would return the same way, in a glorified, physical body:

"all that **Jesus** *began both to do and teach,* **Until the day in which he was taken up,** *after that he through the Holy Ghost had given commandments unto the apostles whom he had chosen: To whom also* **he showed himself alive after his passion by many infallible**

proofs, *being seen of them forty days, and speaking of the things pertaining to the kingdom of God...And when he had spoken these things, while they beheld, he was taken up; and a cloud received him out of their sight. And while they looked steadfastly toward heaven as he went up, behold, two men stood by them in white apparel; Which also said, Ye men of Galilee, why stand ye gazing up into heaven? this same Jesus, which is taken up from you into heaven, shall so come in like manner as ye have seen him go into heaven.* "

Jesus left with His visible, physical, glorified body and He will return with His glorified physical Body. He is still God in the Flesh... He is the Man Christ Jesus. **However, there are some teachers who deny Jesus' Bodily resurrection. They say Jesus was only in the flesh temporarily but now is only spirit.** This is **dangerous heresy.** The Bible states that if you do not confess Jesus is come in the flesh you are a deceiver and an antichrist:

I John 4
[1] Beloved, believe not every spirit, but try the spirits whether they are of God: because many false prophets are gone out into the world. [2] Hereby know ye the Spirit of God: Every spirit that confesses that Jesus Christ is come in the flesh is of God: [3] And every spirit that confesses not that Jesus Christ is come in the flesh is not of God: and this is that spirit of antichrist, whereof ye have heard that it should come; and even now already is it in the world.

II John:
[7] For many deceivers are entered into the world, who confess not that Jesus Christ is come in the flesh. This is a deceiver and an anti-christ. [8] Look to yourselves, that we lose not those things which we have wrought, but that we receive a full reward. [9] Whosoever transgresses, and abides not in the doctrine of Christ, hath not God. He that abides in the doctrine of Christ, he hath both the Father and the Son. [10] If there come any unto you, and bring not this doctrine, receive him not into your house, neither bid him God speed: [11] For he that bids him God speed is partaker of his evil deeds. "

What is the doctrine of Christ? According to Isaiah 9 Jesus Messiah is *one who is born* (man) and *God*:

*"For unto us **a child is born**, unto us a son is given: and the government shall be upon his shoulder: and his name shall be called Wonderful, Counselor, The **mighty God,** The everlasting Father, The Prince of Peace.*

[7] Of the increase of his government and peace there shall be no end, upon the throne of David, and upon his kingdom, to order it, and to establish it with judgment and with justice from henceforth even forever."

This is the definition of the Christ: the Messiah is of the <u>seed of David</u> (man) and is also the <u>Mighty God</u>. To say that Jesus is no longer flesh is antichrist. Paul tells us clearly that Jesus Christ still is genetically "of the seed of David" (as far as His humanity): *"Remember that **Jesus Christ of the seed of David was raised from the dead according to my gospel.** "* (II Timothy 2:8)

He is "the God-man, Christ Jesus*": "For there is one God and one Mediator between God and man, <u>**the Man Christ Jesus**</u>."* (I Timothy 2:5) In Romans 1:3 it states: ***Concerning His <u>Son Jesus Christ our Lord,</u> which <u>was made of the seed of David according to the flesh;</u> [4] And declared to be the Son of God with power, according to the spirit of holiness, <u>by the resurrection from the dead:</u>***

And Jesus Himself testifies (after He had ascended to the right hand of the Majesty on High) that **He was still God and <u>Man</u> by calling Himself "<u>the offspring of David</u>"** in Revelation 22:13-15:

"<u>I am Alpha and Omega</u>, the beginning and the end, the first and the last. Blessed are they that do his commandments, that they may have right to the tree of life, and may enter in through the gates into the city. For without are dogs, and sorcerers, and whoremongers, and murderers, and idolaters, and whosoever loves and makes a lie. <u>I</u>

Jesus have sent mine angel to testify unto you these things in the churches. I am the root and the offspring of David, and the bright and morning star."

In Matthew 24:30 Jesus referred to Himself as the "Son of Man" (title of the Messiah) when He refers to His second coming:

"And then shall appear the sign of the Son of man in heaven: and then shall all the tribes of the earth mourn, and they shall see the Son of man coming in the clouds of heaven with power and great glory."

This confirms that Jesus maintains His identity both as God and Man, both while in Heaven and when He returns to reign on the earth. However, popular Morning Star ministries leader, Rick Joyner, denies this core doctrine of Christianity, saying:

> "There is a tendency to continue relating to Him as **'the MAN from Galilee.' Jesus is not a man. He was and is Spirit.** He took the **form** of a servant and became a man for a brief time."-Rick Joyner, There Were Two Trees in the Garden. New Kensington, Pa.: Whitaker House, 1992, pg. 59; Kindle version Loc 1031 of 3390.

This doctrine is antichrist heresy—the blatant denial that Jesus is in the flesh-all God and all Man. Joyner not only denies that Jesus is God in the Flesh, but also denies the Rapture of the Church. He is wrong on both counts. Thank God that we DO HAVE that blessed hope! As members of His resurrected Body we have the promise that we will be resurrected from the dead also:

"Jesus said unto her, I am the resurrection, and the life: he that believeth in me, though he were dead, yet shall he live. And whosoever lives and believeth in me shall never die." (John 11:25, 26)

The study of the Rapture (resurrection of the living and dead saints at Jesus' coming) is important because it is part of the foundational doctrine of "resurrection from the dead." Hebrews 6:1, 2 tells us that we must have our spiritual foundation laid properly to go on unto spiritual maturity, and it includes properly understanding the resurrection from the dead. Without properly believing in the resurrection of Christ from the dead we cannot even be saved! Paul spent much time writing clarification to the Church so that they would not be confused (I Thes. 1:10; 4:14-18; I Thes. 5:1-11; II Thes. 2:1-17; Titus 2:13,14; I Corinthians 15). Paul warned Timothy that those who deny the resurrection—Rapture— (*saying it was already passed*) were in spiritual error and that false doctrine was like a cancer, overthrowing the faith of some:

*"Study to show thyself approved unto God, a workman that needeth not to be ashamed, **rightly dividing the word of truth.** But shun pro-fane and vain babblings: for they will increase unto more ungodliness. And their word will eat as doth a canker: of whom is Hymenaeus and Philetus; Who **concerning the truth have erred, saying that the resurrection is past already; and overthrow the faith of some.** Nevertheless, the foundation of God stands sure, having this seal, The Lord knows them that are his. And, Let everyone that names the name of Christ depart from **iniquity.**"* (II Timothy 2:16-18.)

Note: here it refers to the believer's resurrection (i.e., the Rapture). Obviously, Christ's resurrection already had past. That is a truth. But the false doctrine that Paul was addressing was to say that the **Church's resurrection** was already past (in the first century.)

There were some in the first century Church who equated the persecution of Caesar with that of the antichrist and taught the believers had missed the Resurrection... that there would be no Rapture of the Church. Perhaps they thought that the Old Testament saints' resurrection (as described in Matthew 27 after Jesus rose from the dead) was the resurrection for the righteous and that they had missed it. They thought that they were experiencing the great tribulation. This false doctrine (i.e., no Rapture) denies the imminent return of Jesus for the saints, and was called by Paul "iniquity" and a spiritual "cancer" that overthrew the faith of the saints. It robbed them of the Blessed Hope of Jesus' return and disillusioned the saints into thinking they were experiencing the wrath of Almighty God. The doctrine of the Rapture is intended to be a source of "good hope, edification, and comfort" (I Thes. 4:18; 5:9-11). It is a motivation for living a holy life (Titus 2:12-14) and will motivate us to be zealous for Jesus: *"steadfast, unmovable, always abounding in the work of the Lord"*- I Cor. 15:54-58.) Seeing the finish line gives motivation to finish the race strong.

The world needs to know that there is an escape from the coming time of tribulation. Many know the Bible predictions of the One World Order government, the antichrist, etc. and they are afraid. Some become reactionary and get a survivalist mentality thinking they must store up enough food and ammunition to ward off the antichrist for seven years. It is not wrong to have some supplies for natural disasters on hand (for they will surely come even before the tribulation) but true believers will not be on earth for the seven-year tribulation and the reign of the anti-Christ. They need to know that God does not lie, and if one receives Jesus as their Lord of their lives they can "watch and pray always and ESCAPE all these things that shall come to pass and stand before the Son of Man." No wonder the devil wants people confused about this doctrine. Only Jesus can deliver from the coming time of tribulation. The Rapture offers people true hope in a world that has no hope.

2.) WHY DOES IT SAY THE ELECT ARE RAPTURED AFTER THE LAST TRUMPET DURING THE GREAT TRIBULATION IN THE BOOK OF REVELATION?

The "elect" during the Great Tribulation are not the present Church, but those who receive Jesus after the Rapture. The 144,000 sealed Jews are the elect at that time, and later when the tribulation saints receive Jesus they are considered "elect." One must "rightly divide the Word of truth" (II Timothy 2:15) and realize that Jesus is addressing different groups at different prophetic times in His prophecy, that spans almost 2,000 years. In Matthew 24 Jesus warns 3 different groups about false Christs and false prophets. The Church is warned in Matthew 24:5, the 144,000 elect Jews are warned in Matthew 24:10-15, and the tribulation saints who must "endure to the end" are also warned in Matthew 24:23, 24.

Some present day Jewish believers (Messianic believers) have not properly "divided" Jesus' prophecy. They have read that which is directed to the 144,000 male, virgin, Jewish evangelists and the tribulation saints (e.g., fleeing Jerusalem, admonitions regarding Sabbath day) and assumed that it is directed to them. However, the Church is already in Heaven before "Jacob's trouble." At the beginning of the tribulation the only "servants of our God" on the earth are the 144,000 male, virgin, Jewish evangelists from the twelve tribes of Israel. They receive Messiah as a result of the preaching of the two witnesses sent from Heaven (Revelation 7:3-8) and are "sealed" by God. They are the only sealed, "elect" Jewish servants of our God on earth at that time. So, one must rightly divide the scriptures in context to know who is actually being addressed. "Elect" believers during the 7-year tribulation does not refer to the Church.

As far as the resurrection "at the last trump" goes, one must understand that there are different types of trumpets sounded for different purposes. In Numbers 10:2-7 it tells us that trumpets sounded for three reasons:

*"And the LORD spoke unto Moses, saying: Make thee two trumpets of silver; of a whole piece shalt thou make them: that thou may use them for the **calling of the assembly, and for the journeying of the camps**. [3] And when they shall blow with them, all the assembly shall assemble themselves to thee at the door of the tabernacle of the congregation. [4] And if they blow but with one trumpet, then the princes, which are heads of the thousands*

of Israel, shall gather themselves unto thee. [5] **When ye blow an alarm**, *then the camps that lie on the east parts shall go forward. [6] When ye blow an alarm the second time, then the camps that lie on the south side shall take their journey: they shall blow an alarm for their journeys.*

[7] But <u>**when**</u> **<u>the congregation is to be gathered together, ye shall blow, but ye shall not sound an alarm.</u>** *[8] And the sons of Aaron, the priests, shall blow with the trumpets; and they shall be to you for an ordinance forever throughout your generations. [9] And* **if ye <u>go to war</u> in your land against the enemy that oppresses you, then ye shall blow an alarm with the trumpets;** *and ye shall be remembered before the LORD your God, and ye shall be saved from your enemies. [10] Also* **in the <u>day of your gladness, and in your solemn days, and in the beginnings of your months, ye</u> shall blow with the trumpets over your burnt offerings,** *and over the sacrifices of your peace offerings; that they may be to you for a memorial before your God: I am the LORD your God.*

One is for "gathering the assembly to take a journey" (the Rapture trumpets of I Thessalonians 4:16 and I Corinthians 15:51 when we are gathered to be with the Lord). The reason I Cor. 15:52 states the "last trumpet" is because the first trumpet causes the dead bodies to rise first (I Thes. 4:16, I Cor. 15:51, 52) and we shall be changed; then at the next (last trump-after the dead bodies are raised) we are all changed, and are "caught up to meet the Lord in the air." In the series of trumpet blasts at the rapture, the initial trump raises the dead, then the last trump causes our bodies to be changed so that we can all rise up to meet the Lord in incorruptible bodies. The first trumpet is to gather the Assembly; the second (last) trumpet is to go on a journey (in this case, Heaven). This is the pre-tribulation resurrection in which trumpet sounds to call us on our heavenly journey.

HOWEVER, there is another purpose for trumpets. It is an alarm to sound for war: Joel 2:1 talks about the Day of the Lord (Jacob's Trouble) and states they should *sound a war alarm*. The trumpet is so that God will save the nation of Israel from her enemies (which corresponds to Matthew 24:31 when Jesus returns at the end of the tribulation to save the Jewish people.)

Those who do not realize there are different purposes for the trumpets assume that the two-part trump of the church to assemble at the Rapture refers to the trumpets of war blown during the tribulation. The trumpets that blow during the tribulation are trumpets of judgment and alarm in a time of war—NOT to go on a heavenly journey as the church does at the pre-tribulation Rapture. The judgment trumpets of war are that which are sounded during the tribulation period, which is different from the gathering trumpets sounded at the Rapture.)

3.) ISN'T THE RAPTURE A NEW, MAN-MADE DOCTRINE OF "ESCAPE" THEOLOGY?

The doctrine of the Pre-tribulation Rapture is CLEARLY taught by the **Word of God**, so **NO**, it is not *NEW*. The apostles and Jesus taught it, so it is almost 2,000 years old. But, YES... *IT IS* **ESCAPE** THEOLOGY. But **it is not man-made doctrine**. **Jesus promised escape**:

*"WATCH AND PRAY ALWAYS SO THAT YOU CAN **ESCAPE ALL THESE THINGS THAT SHALL COME TO PASS AND STAND BEFORE THE SON OF MAN.**"* (Luke 21:36)

Jesus also states:

"I WILL COME AGAIN AND RECEIVE YOU TO MYSELF THAT WHERE I AM [HEAVEN] YOU MAY BE ALSO" (John 14:1-3)

*"I WILL **KEEP YOU FROM** THE HOUR OF TEMPTATION THAT SHALL COME ON ALL THE WORLD TO TRY THEM THAT DWELL UPON THE EARTH."* (Revelation 3)

Paul the Apostle also taught it: "GOD HAS NOT APPOINTED US TO WRATH [tribulation wrath]" The Word of God does not contradict. The doctrine of the pre-tribulation rapture is based on the inerrant, inspired, Word of God. As II Timothy 3:16 states, *"All scripture is given by inspiration of God, and is profitable for doctrine, for reproof, for correction, for instruction in righteousness."*

Our doctrine cannot be based on a vision, prophecy, dream or any other experience. We must "test all things" by Holy Scripture. To get a complete understanding of a doctrine one must take all of the Scripture on a particular topic into consideration (not dismissing any) and keep the scripture in context. The foremost consideration of any doctrine is whether or not it is scriptural. If it contradicts any part of scripture, it cannot be true.

Of late there has been a tendency for people to disregard the scripture based on an experience, dream, vision, etc. Isaiah 8:20 says, *"If they speak not according to the Law and the testimony they have no light in them."* II Timothy says ALL scripture is profitable for doctrine... therefore one cannot dismiss ANY scripture on any given topic. One must take ALL scripture on a matter to know the truth. Jesus said, "You shall know the truth and the truth shall make you free.

4.) DIDN'T JESUS SAY WE WOULD SUFFER TRIBULATION?

Jesus said, *"In this world you shall suffer tribulation."* He meant that Christians throughout the ages will suffer trials and tribulations as they strive to live godly and righteous lives in an unrighteous world— that they shall suffer persecution, rejection, spoiling of their goods, and some even martyrdom from those who reject Christ. The persecution comes *from the world.* However, THE Great Tribulation is when GOD POURS OUT HIS WRATH on the ungodly. Christians *"are not appointed to experience God's wrath."*

The Smyrna church was certainly representative of a suffering

Body of believers during the church age of grace. But Paul clearly admonishes the church of Thessalonica (who were experiencing persecution: I Thes.1:6; 5:9) that they could look forward to *"Jesus which delivers us from the wrath to come."* Christians will suffer persecution from demon inspired people if they are living right, but it is *not God's wrath.*

In II Thessalonians 1:4-10 Paul tells the Church that they should be encouraged because God is going to *"take vengeance on those who persecute them"* and pay them back with TRIBULATION w h e n Jesus comes. But the Church is going to REST when the Lord Jesus is revealed from Heaven. Christians may be called to suffer for the Kingdom of God's sake at the hands of the devil-inspired people. However, that is not the same as experiencing the *WRATH* of <u>God</u>.

God's wrath is reserved <u>for His enemies</u>, the children of disobedience (Nahum 1:2, Colossians 3:6). God's wrath begins at the beginning of the 7-year time of "Jacob's Trouble." Rev. 6:17 states that at the time the seals are opened (the first set of judgments) it is ALREADY considered the day of *wrath*: *"for the great day of His wrath is come, and who shall be able to stand."* Though the latter half of the tribulation is worse than the first half, it is all a time when God is pouring out His wrath upon *"those that <u>dwell on the face of the whole earth</u>."* (Isaiah 26:19-21) The comfort for believers is *"God has not appointed us for wrath, but for deliverance through our Lord Jesus Christ."* (I Thessalonians 5:9)

Post tribulation negates Jesus own words that state: *"In My Father's house are many mansions. I go to prepare a place for you, and if I go and prepare a place for you [in Heaven] I will come again and receive to Myself that where I am [Heaven] you may be also."* (John 14:1-3) He did not say 'I'm going to come and join you down on the earth.' He said He would *receive us to Himself that where He is-- in Heaven-- we may be also.*

The pre-tribulation (pre-indignation) Rapture is clearly depicted in Isaiah 26:19-21: "your dead men shall live" (resurrection); "come My people, enter into your chambers [mansions]" (catching up to heaven); "until God's indignation (wrath) is overpast, for the Lord is coming out of His place to punish the inhabitants of the earth." The **inhabitants of the earth are punished**, but not God's people who are hidden in their Heavenly chambers.

Luke 21:34-36 confirms this stating Christians should take heed to themselves LEST they are not ready (overcharged with surfeiting, drunkenness, and cares of this life so that day comes on them unaware.) "For as a snare it shall come on all them that **dwell on the face of the whole earth**. Watch and pray always that you may be able to ESCAPE all these things and stand before the Son of Man."

It's conditional. If you don't watch you won't be ready for His coming and that day WILL come upon them unexpectedly. But if you do watch and pray, you will escape and will not be on the earth to experience God's wrath. Rev. 3:10 clearly states that because the true Church of Philadelphia had not denied His name and kept His Word, *"I will also keep you from the hour of temptation* [tribulation] *that shall come upon all the world to try them that dwell upon the earth*. True believers will not be on the earth: they will be in Heaven.

To think that Christians will not suffer is not taught by God's Word. We should expect suffering at the hands of the ungodly. There will be persecution before the Church is Raptured, but it will NOT be God's wrath they experience, but the enemy's persecution.

If true believers who are ready for Jesus experience God's wrath ("the Day of the Lord") then Jesus lied. He said that if believers would watch and pray, they would **escape it all.** But Jesus *did not* lie! It is impossible for Him to lie. Therefore, there is a group that escapes the wrath to come: the Church in the pre-tribulation Rapture.

However, after the Rapture, God's focus then shifts to the nation of Israel to fulfill Daniel's 70th week, the "time of Jacob's trouble" (Jeremiah 30:7). At that time, He then "seals" His new group of "elect," (that is, the 144,000 male, virgin Jews). According to Revelation 7:3 they are the **only** "Servants of our God" on the earth at that time. That precludes any married male Jew or Gentile and all women as being His servants on the earth. That is because the Church is not on the earth. The only "elect" at the beginning of the tribulation are God's servants, the 144,000 literal Jewish evangelists. They are "sealed" and do not have to experience God's wrath as others on earth do (Rev. 9:4).

The prophecies of Jesus MUST be divided properly to understand who Jesus is actually addressing: "Study to show yourself approved unto God, a workman that needs not to be ashamed, *rightly dividing* the Word of Truth." (II Timothy 2:15) Here Paul is addressing wrong teaching about the Rapture, and how to avoid error: "Rightly divide the Word of Truth" so that you understand what Jesus is saying, and to whom.

The true Church may suffer persecution from the ungodly, but *will not suffer God's wrath* during the day of the Lord.

Book of Revelation Outline

The Book of Revelation is very clear about the order of prophetic events. Jesus Himself outlines the book of the Revelation for us:

"Write the things that you have seen" (past-tense, the glorified Christ), as seen in Revelation 1.	*"The things that are"* (present tense, the church age symbolized by the 7 churches in Rev. 2 & 3.	*"The things that shall be hereafter"* (future tense, what occurs after the church age- Rev. 4-19.)

John represents the Church being raptured when he hears "Come up here" and goes through the open door to heaven in Chapter 4. From that point on, the Church is only depicted in Heaven until the end of the seven-year time of tribulation on earth. Notice that John sees 24 elders in heaven before God's throne with crowns on their heads in Revelation 4. Crowns are not given until the Church is caught up to Heaven when Jesus appears at the Rapture. (II Timothy 2:5; 4:7,8; I Peter 5:4; Rev. 3:11; I Thes. 2:19) Once the Church is in Heaven, the seals are opened and God's wrath is released upon the earth (Revelation 6:17).

To say scripture does not teach a pre-tribulation Rapture is incorrect. Jesus said to watch because His coming is imminent. Those who are ready will "***escape all these things*** *and stand before the Son of Man.*" To say no theologians believed that Christians would escape the tribulation is wrong. It has been a basic doctrine of the church since Jesus spoke it, Matthew, Mark, Luke, and John recorded it, and the Apostle Paul clarified it. It is the blessed hope... the appearing of our Lord Jesus Christ.

All scripture has been preserved by God Almighty, and the Greek manuscripts confirm that we have the right Bible. We can trust what the Bible teaches concerning prophecy. Remember: "All scripture is given by inspiration of God, and is profitable for doctrine, for reproof, for correction, for instruction in righteousness." The Holy Bible is the final Word. It preempts any prophecy, vision, dream, tradition, theology, or opinion.

10 REASONS sATAN HATES THE RAPTURE DOCTRINE

1. The Rapture is the bodily resurrection of Christians at Jesus' coming. Faith in resurrection of Christ's Body (which includes the Church at the RAPTURE) is how we are justified: **Romans 4:22-5:1** *"And therefore it was imputed to him for righteousness. Now it was not written for his sake alone, that it was imputed to him; But for us also, to whom it shall be imputed, if we believe on him that raised up Jesus our Lord from the dead; Who was delivered for our offences, and was raised again for our justification. Therefore being justified by faith, we have peace with God through our Lord Jesus Christ."* In **John 14:19** Jesus said, *"Because I live, you shall live also."*

2. The antichrist spirit denies Jesus in the flesh, and His returning to raise His Body at Rapture (**1 John 4:1-3**) *"Beloved, believe not every spirit, but try the spirits whether they are of God: because many false prophets are gone out into the world.[2] Hereby know ye the Spirit of God: Every spirit that confesses that Jesus Christ is come in the flesh is of God: And every spirit that confesses not that Jesus Christ is come in the flesh is not of God: and this is that spirit of antichrist, whereof ye have heard that it should come; and even now already is it in the world."* If Jesus does not have a body, then we cannot be resurrected. **Acts 1:11** *"This same Jesus will return in like manner as you have seen Him go."* Jesus left in a glorified, physical BODY. In John 2, Jesus clearly states it was His physical body that was raised from the dead: *"destroy this temple and in 3 days I will raise it up"* (speaking His body). However, false teachers state that Jesus is only spirit. Romans 8 tells us *"If the Spirit of Him that raised up Jesus from the dead* [bodily] *dwells in you, He that raised up Christ from the dead shall also quicken* [make alive at the Rapture] *your mortal bodies by His Spirit that dwells in you."*

3. **I Cor. 15: 12-27**: The Rapture shows that Jesus is risen and will return personally to reign. JESUS establishes His own kingdom and reigns (*not* NAR "apostles"): ***"Now if Christ be preached that he rose from the dead, how say some among you that there is no resurrection of the dead? But if there be no resurrection of the dead, then is Christ not risen:*** *And if Christ be not risen, then is our preaching vain, and your faith is also vain. Yea, and we are found false witnesses of God; because we have testified of God that he raised up Christ: whom he raised not up, if so be that the dead rise not. For if the dead rise not, then is not Christ raised:* ***And if Christ be not raised, your faith is vain; ye are yet in your sins.*** *Then they also which are fallen asleep in Christ are perished. If in this life only we have hope in Christ, we are of all men most miserable.* ***But now is Christ risen from the dead,*** *and become the firstfruits of them that slept. For since by man came death, by man came also the resurrection of the dead. For as in Adam all die, even so in Christ shall all be made alive. But every man in his own order: Christ the firstfruits; afterward they that are Christ's at his coming.* ***Then cometh the end, when He shall have delivered up the kingdom to God, even the Father; when*** <u>***HE***</u> ***SHALL HAVE PUT DOWN ALL RULE AND ALL AUTHORITY AND POWER."***

4. **Philippians 3:10-4:1** The Rapture doctrine causes the Church to stand fast in the Lord: *"That I may know Him, and the power of His resurrection, and the fellowship of His sufferings, being made conformable unto His death; If by any means I might* **attain unto the resurrection of the dead**... *For our conversation is in* **heaven; from whence also** <u>**we look for the Savior, the Lord Jesus Christ:**</u> *Who shall change our vile body* [at the Rapture], *that it may be fashioned like unto his glorious body, according to the working whereby he is able even to subdue all things unto himself...* **Therefore,** *my brethren dearly beloved and longed for, my joy and crown,* <u>**so stand fast in the Lord**</u>, *my dearly beloved.*

5.   **I Cor. 15:51-58** The truth of the Rapture causes the Church to abound in the work of the Lord: *"**In a moment, in the twinkling of an eye, at the last trump: for the trumpet shall sound, and the dead shall be raised incorruptible, and we shall be changed.** For this corruptible must put on incorruption, and this mortal must put on immortality. So when this corruptible shall have put on incorruption, and this mortal shall have put on immortality, then shall be brought to pass the saying that is written, Death is swallowed up in victory... But thanks be to God, which giveth us **the victory through our Lord Jesus Christ. <u>Therefore, my beloved brethren, be ye steadfast, unmoveable, always abounding in the work of the Lord,</u>** forasmuch as ye know that your labor is not in vain in the Lord."*

6.   The truth of the Rapture causes us to live Godly, pure lives. See **Titus 2:12-14**: *"For the grace of God that brings salvation hath appeared to all men, Teaching us that, **denying ungodliness and worldly lusts, we should live soberly, righteously, and godly, in this present world; Looking for that blessed hope, and the glorious appearing of the great God and our Savior Jesus Christ;** Who gave himself for us, that he might redeem us from all iniquity, and purify unto himself a peculiar people, zealous of good works."*

    John confirms the purifying effect of the Rapture in **I John 3:2, 3:** *"Beloved, now are we the sons of God, and it doth not yet appear what we shall be: but we know that, **when he shall appear, we shall be like him; for we shall see him as he is. And every man that hath this hope in him purifies himself, even as he is pure.**"*

7.   The truth of the Rapture is actually spiritual armor for the believer (i.e., the "helmet of salvation."), **I Thes. 5:8-10**. *"But let us, who are of the day, be sober, putting on the breastplate of faith and love; **and for an helmet, the hope of salvation. For God hath not appointed us to wrath, but to obtain salvation** (the context means *"deliverance"* from the

7-year time of God's wrath) *by our Lord Jesus Christ, Who died for us, that, whether we wake or sleep, we should live together with him."* (**Ephesians 6:13**) Wherefore take unto you the <u>whole armor of God</u>, that ye may be able to withstand in the evil day, and having done all, to stand… take the …**helmet of salvation.**

8. The Rapture is a source of comfort for believers, knowing that their loved ones who die in the Lord will rise again. It is also a comfort to know that the church is not destined for the Day of Lord's wrath (**I Thes. 4:14-18**): *"For if we believe that Jesus died and rose again, even so them also which sleep in Jesus will God bring with him. For this we say unto you by the word of the Lord, that we which are alive and remain unto the coming of the Lord shall not prevent them which are asleep. For the Lord himself shall descend from heaven with a shout, with the voice of the archangel, and with the trump of God: and the dead in Christ shall rise first: Then we which are alive and remain shall be **caught up** together with them in the clouds, to meet the Lord in the air: and so shall we ever be with the Lord. Wherefore **comfort one another with these words."***

 Also, **I Thes. 5:9-11** says: ***"For God hath not appointed us to wrath, but to obtain salvation by our Lord Jesus Christ, Who died for us, that, whether we wake or sleep*** [at the Rapture] ***we should live together with him. Wherefore comfort yourselves together, and edify one another, even as also ye do."***

9. The Rapture (the resurrection of believers) is foundational teaching necessary for spiritual maturity. False teaching that denies the Rapture is called spiritual cancer. **Hebrews 6:1, 2** states: *"Therefore leaving **the principles of the doctrine of Christ, let us go on unto perfection**; not laying again the foundation of repentance from dead works, and of faith toward God, Of the doctrine of baptisms, and of laying on of hands, and of **resurrection of the dead**, and of eternal judgment."*

It tells us in **II Timothy 2:15-19** that those who teach against the imminent coming of Jesus (deny the Rapture) are vain babblers: *"But shun profane and vain babblings: for they will increase unto more ungodliness. And their word will eat as doth a canker: of whom is Hymenaeus and Philetus;* **Who concerning the truth have erred, saying that the resurrection (Rapture) is past already; and overthrow the faith of some.** *Nevertheless the foundation of God stands sure, having this seal, The Lord knows them that are his. And, Let every one that names the name of Christ depart from iniquity."*

10.   The Pretribulation Rapture teaching is hated by satan because it causes God's people to be watching and ready for Jesus' return (**Hebrews 9:27, 28**): *"And as it is appointed unto men once to die, but after this the judgment: So Christ was once offered to bear the sins of many; and* **unto them that** <u>*look for Him*</u> **shall He appear the second time without sin unto salvation.** *"* Jesus tells us in **Luke 21:36**: ***<u>Watch ye therefore, and pray always, that ye may be accounted worthy to escape all these things</u> that shall come to pass, and to stand before the Son of man."***

Because the Pre-tribulation Rapture of the Church assures true believers that they will escape the tribulation time, gives believers hope and good comfort, and motivates believers to Godly living, purity, and service to the Lord, it is a hated doctrine of the devil. That is why he fights the truth and tries to bring confusion to the Body of Christ. Jesus is coming soon, and His reward is with Him. It's time to "look up!"

REFERENCE STUDY: DREAMS OF DANIEL

There are several dreams and visions of the apocalyptic nature in the book of Daniel. This study will discuss two dreams found in chapters 2 and 7. Daniel Chapter 2 begins with Nebuchadnezzar, the king of Babylon, having a prophetic dream. Nebuchadnezzar was troubled by the dream, for he knew it was significant, but could not remember what the dream actually was. Daniel, a captive Jewish prophet, was shown the dream and given the interpretation by God. Upon sharing the dream and interpretation with the king, Daniel was promoted in the kingdom. Nebuchadnezzar acknowledged the God of Daniel as "the God of gods Who reveals secrets." What was the dream that Daniel interpreted? What the king had seen was a great image or idol made of various metals. "This image's head was of fine gold, his breast and his arms of silver, his belly and thighs of brass, his legs of iron, his feet part of iron and part of clay." vs. 32, 33. A stone cut without hands struck the image and destroyed it. The stone then became a great mountain and filled the whole earth.

The interpretation given to Daniel was that the golden head of the image symbolized Nebuchadnezzar and the glorious Babylonian Kingdom. His dominion was over all peoples of the world. The silver chest and arms symbolized a kingdom not quite as glorious as Babylon that would arise in Babylon's stead. This describes the Medio-Persian Empire. The two arms indicate two spheres of power in this joint Medes and Persian kingdom. The third world power to arise was the Greek empire. Alexander the Great supplanted the Medio-Persian Empire in his zeal to conquer the world. The brass symbolized the Greek Empire as being inferior in glory to the previous silver kingdom of the Medes and Persians. However, the Greek empire would still "bear rule over all the earth." (v.39) The fourth kingdom "shall be strong as iron." This was the Roman Empire. Since Rome was primarily known for its military might and power, iron was a fitting symbol. The two iron legs represented the Eastern and Western Roman empires.

After the iron legs were feet and toes of iron mixed with clay. This symbolized a futuristic extension of the Roman Empire, in that the element iron is still used. But the fact that it is mixed with clay indicates this futuristic empire would not have the solid unity as had the historic Roman Empire. Rather, the mixture of iron and clay indicate strength, but still some autonomy maintained in the various members of the empire (v. 42). The nations of this last day, revived Roman Empire would maintain their nationalistic identity, but would "mingle" (or associate freely) with the other member nations (v. 43). The ten toes indicate 10 "kings" (rulers of spheres of power) within the bounds of the Old Holy Roman Empire which unite as a world power. An obvious present-day fulfillment of this is the European Union (the "EU"). They freely mingle with member nations (no tariffs or visas), but still maintain their national identity. They have a common currency (the "Euro"). And, these entities are within the bounds of the Old Holy Roman Empire. The 10 toes of the vision could be similar to the 10 voting member nations of the former Western European Union's (WEU) Security Council. These ten members had authority over the military issues of the WEU. They were not necessarily "kings" of separate countries, but rather, ten that had spheres of military influence or dominion.) A future 10-member confederacy will eventually "give their power" to the anti-Christ when he arises to pursue world domination. (Rev. 17:12, 13.)

The stage is set for the European Union to receive this political and economic "hero." Many Europeans are calling for centralized leadership for the EU. The exciting part of this scenario is that "*in the days of these kings (EU leaders) shall the God of heaven set up a kingdom which shall never be destroyed.*" (v.44) In other words, the leaders of these member nations will still be in power when Jesus returns to set up His Kingdom! The prophetic stage is set. Jesus' coming is soon. First, He will "catch away" (rapture) His Church to heaven (I Thes. 4:14-18). After that is the 7-year rule of the anti-Christ. Then Jesus returns with His Church to set up His earthly kingdom. This will all be fulfilled "in the days *of these kings.*"

In summary, this dream's interpretation shows a historical, panoramic view of the world's four great empires—Babylon, Medio-Persia, Greece, and Rome. In each case the ruling empire was supplanted by the subsequent world empire. However, the EU (the revived Roman Empire, symbolized by iron and clay) is considered an extension of the ancient Roman Empire, and so did not supplant it. It is part of the fourth "iron" kingdom.

The dream of Daniel Chapter 7 is often times compared to that of Chapter 2. In fact, because of many similarities, many interpret the two dreams as being one in the same (that is, the four historical world empires mentioned before.) However, there are some very important distinctions. The main difference is that Ch. 2 deals primarily with historical empires, and Ch. 7 discusses contemporary world powers. In both cases, however, the dreams culminate with the destruction of the anti-Christ's domain and Jesus establishing His Kingdom on earth. In comparing the dreams, the first obvious difference is that of the symbolism. Chapter 2 compares the world kingdoms to various types of metals. Chapter 7 also deals with four world powers, but they are represented by different types of beasts.

Another important difference is that the four kingdoms of Ch. 2 exist at different periods of time, historically spanning hundreds of years. One kingdom succeeds the other (Medo-Persia following Babylonian, for example). The domains of power in Ch. 7 exist simultaneously, and in different geographical areas. When Daniel wrote the dreams, both Babylon and the Medes and Persian powers were established. (He wrote one during Nebuchadnezzar's reign, and one during Belshazzar's reign-7:1.) Belshazzar was the last king of Babylon to reign before Darius the Mede took over (Daniel 5:30, 31.) But in interpreting the identity of the four beasts of Ch. 7, Daniel was told these are four kings or dominions which "*SHALL* arise out of the earth" (Dan. 7:16, 17.) Obviously, the four beasts cannot be the same dominions of Chapter 2. They are futuristic kingdoms that exist concurrently.

Both dreams describe the anti-Christ's kingdom taking over the world. But in Chapter 2, the three previous world powers do not exist at the time of the anti-Christ dominion. However, in Daniel 7:7, it discusses how the anti-Christ overtakes the three other world powers (beasts). These kingdoms continue to exist, though absorbed into the anti-Christ's dominion. As soon as the anti-Christ is destroyed (7:11, 12), these three kingdoms are allowed to again exist as separate entities. Most obviously, Babylon, Medes & Persia, Greece and Ancient Rome do not fit into this scenario. They did not exist concurrently as world powers, and no longer exist for the anti-Christ to take them over in the last days.

What are the identities, then, of the four beasts (kingdoms) mentioned in Daniel Chapter 7? The fourth beast's identity is easy to interpret. Daniel 7:7 states that the fourth beast has 10 horns. Revelation 13:1 describes a beast with 10 horns that is the kingdom over which the anti-Christ reigns. These ten horns correspond to the 10 toes of Chapter 2 (ten countries/spheres of power) in the bounds of the old Holy Roman Empire.)

So, the fourth beast is the domain of the European Union over which the anti-Christ will rule. This power eventually overtakes three other global powers and then, all the world. Daniel 7:7 describes the 4th beast as having "teeth of iron." This is further indication that the 4th beast represents the revived Roman Empire, since iron is the element used to represent Rome in Ch. 2. The EU countries began to unite in 1957 under the "Treaty of Rome," which encouraged Western European countries to trade and establish closer ties and unity.

The power base from which the anti-Christ will reign is the EU, established Jan. 1, 1993. Because the three other beasts (kingdoms) exist concurrently with this fourth beast (the EU), the other kingdoms are dominions which must exist today as well. Their identities can be ascertained by comparing scripture and historical facts. Here is Daniel's description of the beasts in 7:2, 3:

"Daniel spoke and said, I saw in my vision by night, and, behold, the four winds of the heaven strove upon the great sea. And four great beasts come up from the sea, diverse one from another."

Firstly, the "four winds of the heaven" are mentioned. Since satan is called the "prince of the power of the air" (Ephesians 2:2) and we "wrestle against spiritual wickedness in high places" (Eph. 6:12), it seems evident that these are demonic spirits. These spirits seem to control the emergence of the 4 beasts (dominions of world power.) These could correspond to the same demonic angels which are loosed in Rev. 9:14, 15, and to the 4 demonic spirits of destruction mentioned in Zech. 6:5. In any case, these 4 spirits over the 4 beasts (spheres of power) were striving over the great sea (v. 2) These four great beasts come up from the sea (v.3). According to Revelation 13:1 and Rev. 17:15, the "sea" represents "peoples, and multitudes, and nations, and tongues." These beasts are dominions which come from the various peoples and nations of the world and are different from one another.

The first beast emerges in verse 4: "The first was like a lion, and had eagle's wings: I beheld till the wings thereof were plucked, and it was lifted up from the earth, and made stand upon the feet as a man, and a man's heart was given to it." Notice the word "first." God is giving us the chronological order in which these dominions emerge. The lion with eagle's wings is the first dominion to become an established power. What does the "lion" represent? According to Ezekiel 38:13, Spain and its colonized lands are called lions: "and the merchants of Tarshish, [famous trade city of Spain] with all the young lions thereof." Here we see that the colonized lands of Spain—the offspring or "young lions"—are symbolized by a lion. It is not coincidental that Spain's state flag bears the emblem of a lion on its coat of arms. And so, given only the "lion" clue alone, it seems that Spain or the new lands it colonized is inferred here. When the lion symbol is combined with the "eagle's wings, it becomes evident that the new world, (the Western Hemisphere including the United States) is the proper interpretation.

The New World democracies were originally discovered and colonized by Spain, and can be symbolized by the "lion." The "eagle's wings" represent the United States, whose national emblem is the bald eagle. The fact that these are mentioned show that the US is a prominent member of the New World (Western democracies) Dominion. This Western sphere of power could be fulfilled in NAFTA (the North American Free Trade Agreement.) Although the US and its other Western Hemisphere neighbors have had trade relationships for some time now, they were not considered a world trading entity. But, in order to compete with the EU, they have officially united as a world trade power under the NAFTA agreement. This union of New World countries into a powerful trading alliance seems to fulfill the symbol of the lion with eagle's wings "kingdom."

One disconcerting aspect of verse 4 is the phrase "the wings there-of were plucked." Since plucking an eagle's wings would result in its ultimate death, it is evident that the eagle is going to incur severe, if not deadly, judgment.

Many find it hard to believe that God could allow the United States ("one nation under God") to be judged. America was founded on God's Word and the principles thereof. However, to whom much is given, much is required. God expects more righteousness and truth in America where the Gospel has had free reign. But, rather than growing closer to God, America has degenerated socially, morally and spiritually despite of all the exposure to the Gospel.

Obviously, there are many dedicated Christians in the US, but the majority of the people have rejected God to follow their own lusts. In His love, God will allow judgment to fall to draw them to repentance. That is the pattern He used throughout the Old Testament when dealing with Israel's rebellion. Christians can and should pray for judgment to be averted or delayed, but when rebellion has festered to a certain point, judgment is inevitable. Indications of the "point of no return" are blatant homosexuality (Gen 18, 19), and disregard for human life, especially innocent babies and children (Jeremiah 32:35). Christians can claim II Chronicles 7:14 for their individual "land" and Psalm 91 for protection, even if the world around them must be judged.

There are other indications in scripture that America will be judged. One significant point is that nowhere in the book of Revelation is the United States alluded to, though the other world powers are specifically mentioned. It is an ominous sign that a country of the magnitude of the United States is not mentioned; indicating it no longer is significant politically, economically, or militarily.

Isaiah 18 indicates judgment to "the land shadowing with wings." It is a land "across the sea", from Israel (which eliminates Europe, Asia, and Africa from fulfilling this description.) The land "shadowing with wings" is exactly how America depicts its emblem, the bald eagle, with its out-stretched wings on currency and coins, etc.

Another indication of the eagle's wings being plucked" (judgment on America) is found in Ezekiel chapter 39. The preceding chapter deals with Israel back in their land in the "latter days", v. 16. This is fulfilled now. Then it describes how Russian and Arab nations allied together would attack Israel during a time of pseudo-peace (38:11.) As the Word of God clearly states, when they shall cry "peace and safety" (the two main tenets of any peace treaty being proposed for Israel and its militant Arab neighbors), there would be "sudden destruction." (I Thes. 5:1, 2)

God will supernaturally come to Israel's aid, and the Russians and their allies will be routed. In the context of this surprise attack on Israel, an interesting verse appears:

"And I will send a fire on Magog, and among them that dwell carelessly in the isles: and they shall know that I am the Lord." (Ezekiel 39:6)

The term "isles" in the Hebrew can also be translated "desirable land." God says that fire will fall on the "desirable land which dwells carelessly." Of all countries of the world, the United States is considered the most desirable: it is the land of opportunity to which all refugees desire to flee. The fact that this land is dwelling "carelessly" indicates it is far away from--and not involved in-- the Russia/Israeli War (which encompasses nations from Europe, the Middle East, and Africa.)

America signed an agreement with Russia in Jan. 1994 to no longer point their nuclear missiles at each other. This has given America a false sense of security and a mentality that the "cold war is over." However, Ezekiel 38, 39 indicate that Russia is not the peace-loving nation it portrays itself as being, but is ready and willing to attack innocent targets unexpectedly. Given Russia's track record on keeping peace treaties it has signed, the "peace and safety" mentality of the United States may set it up for "sudden destruction." (I Thessalonians 5:3.)

God says that those who dwell in the desirable land without

concern of war would have fire fall upon them (nuclear weapons?) This period of Russian aggression occurs in the "latter days," but apparently before the 7-year tribulation, as there is no mention of it at all in the book of the Revelation. This adds credibility to the United States "Babylon" judgment prior to the Great Tribulation.

One of the first things that anti-Christ does at the beginning of the 7-year tribulation is to negotiate a covenant (probably a peace treaty) with Israel that will allow the Jews to offer sacrifice on Temple Mount. The fact that Israel is currently calling for President Trump and Vladimir Putin to help them build the third Temple is an ominous sign of the time. The Temple Mount committee is ready and willing to get the temple built. The "Kosher" altar upon which the Kohen (priests) will begin temple sacrifice has been in place since 2014. All the implements of the Third Temple are ready... all of the priestly garments, altar of incense, the table of showbread... They are just waiting for the green light to start Temple worship. The surrounding Muslim nations consider any activity on Temple Mount by the Jews as a provocation. The regional Middle East war described in Psalm 83 could happen at any time.

Following that conflict will be the Ezekiel 38 war, with Russia, Iran, Turkey, Libya and other Muslim countries attacking Israel (but being Divinely routed). The fact that a treaty (covenant) allowing for Israel to sacrifice on Temple Mount is signed at the beginning of the 7-year time of "Jacob's Trouble," seems to indicate that those conflicts have already occurred (hence the need to avert any additional conflicts with a covenant between Israel and her antagonistic neighbors.) The nations of the world will support a leader who can bring peace to the Middle East. When the dust of war settles, the anti-Christ comes on the scene with his persuasive "flatteries" and *By peace he will destroy many.*[119] With the momentum of his peace initiative, the anti-christ will quickly rise to

---

[119] Daniel 8:25

world-wide power and prominence. He will wield so much influence that his EU powerbase will boast "Who can make war with him!"[120]

The scenario, therefore, is set. The prophesied wars are imminent. Unfortunately, those wars will precipitate the fire falling on the *"desirable land...in the latter days."*[121] Russia is not the only threat to the United States. North Korea is also a player with no qualms about airing its intentions to attack the land *"shadowing with eagle's wings."* These scriptures seem to point to judgment coming soon upon the United States. God help us to obey Joel 2:15-32, and call for ministers and believers to repent, fast, and pray for our land!

After the wings of the eagle are plucked, the lion stands upon its feet as a man and a "man's heart" was given to it. The term "man" in this chapter refers to the anti-Christ (v. 8.) The fact that a "man's heart" was given to the Western confederacy of nations could indicate their desire toward the anti-Christ's system and alignment with the EU. If America is weakened or destroyed, the Western nations would likely gravitate toward the EU for political, economic and military security.

Continuing on, Daniel 7, verse 5 says: "And behold another beast, a second, like to a bear, and it raised up itself on one side, and it had three ribs in the mouth of it between the teeth of it: and they said thus unto it, Arise, devour much flesh." This second beast is represented by a bear. The "kingdom" (v. 23) or dominion represented by the bear in these latter days is Russia. God knew 2,600 years ago what symbols the latter-day countries would be known by, and incorporated them into Daniel's prophecy for our understanding. The Russian bear is flexing its military might, infiltrating Ukraine, Syria, Libya, and Egypt.

The Russian bear under Communism devoured "much flesh" ruthlessly, conquering many peoples and lands since its inception in 1917. The 3 ribs could indicate three geographical regions into which

---

[120] Revelation
[121] Ezekiel 38:8, 39:9

the Russian influence has spread (Eastern Europe, Asia, & Africa.) Though Communism was officially abolished in Russia, the post-Communist Russia still has many elements of the Communist regime in place. Many of the present leaders and security forces are former KGB elite. Freedom of religion is quickly eroding so that only state sanctioned religious entities can operate. Russia's aggressive agenda to "arise and devour much flesh" will foment the attack with Muslim nations against Israel in these "latter days." God Himself will step in to defend Israel, destroying 5/6^{ths} of the attacking forces.

After the lion (Western powers) and the bear (Russia and its allies), another kingdom, or domain is described. This third world power is represented by a leopard (Daniel 7:6): *"After this I beheld, and lo another, like a leopard, which had upon the back of it four wings of a fowl; the beast had also four heads; and dominion was given to it."* The term "after" indicates after the first two powers (lion & bear) are established, another world power comes on the scene.

The term "leopard" is used here. "Leopard" could indicate that this world power arises quickly. The term "leopard" is "namer" in Hebrew (Strong's #5246.) The word "namer" is derived from terms meaning to "spot" or stain as if by dripping; (from its stripes)." Jer.13:23 says: "shall a leopard (#5246) change his spots." The term spots (#2272) is "a streak (like a line), as on the tiger." The point here is that where the term "leopard" is used, it is actually describing a tiger, and can accurately be translated as such. "Namer" can be correctly translated leopard or "tiger."

The fact that both of these cats are indigenous to Asia gives us a clue to the location of this third, end-time sphere of power (kingdom). Asia has only recently emerged as a world trade power. The Nov. 22, 1993 edition of US News and World Report states: "Rapid growth and industrialization have leapt... to the 'Four Tigers'- Singapore, Taiwan, Hong Kong and South Korea."

It is possible that Daniel saw the four-headed "namer" (tiger) representing the Asian powers. (Daniel 12:9.) Along with the Four Tigers, four other prominent countries have arisen (perhaps the "4 wings of a fowl"?) These are Thailand, Indonesia, Malaysia, and China. Along with the Four Tigers, these countries have become members of a very powerful trading bloc called APEC (Asian Pacific Economic Cooperation.) This Asian trade dominion was established in 1989 (US N.&W.R., Nov.22, 1993.)

According to Revelation 16:12, there is a union of leaders from Asia ("the kings of the East"). This economic cooperation has bought about strong ties between these "kings of the East." Eventually, they will join military forces and come against Israel. Daniel 7:6 states "dominion was given to it." The term "dominion" (Strong's # 7985) means "empire." These Asian "Kings of the East" have an economic empire that eventually will result in their military cooperation. They will gather to fight at Armageddon.[122]

To sum it up, the first three beasts can be interpreted as follows: the lion with eagle's wings symbolizes a Western confederacy with the United States as a prominent member for a time. The bear represents Russia and her allies. The 4-headed "namer" (tiger) represents the Asian "kings of the East." The fourth beast is the revived Roman Empire (also known as the European Union).

Daniel 7:7 states: "After this I saw in the night visions, and behold a fourth beast, dreadful and terrible, and strong exceedingly; and it had great iron teeth: it devoured and broke in pieces, and stamped the residue with the feet of it: and it was diverse from all the beasts that were before it; and it had ten horns." "After" the other three dominions are in place, the anti-Christ will come into power over the EU. This beast is "strong exceedingly," which is not surprising

---

[122] Revelation 16:12

since combined European armies would make for a very formidable military force. The EU worship the "god of forces," and are so proud of their military power, they say: "who is like the beast? who can make war against him?" (Rev. 13:4)

The phrase, *"iron* teeth," again alludes to the military strength of Rome. The *"teeth"* indicate that--along with the military might-- the anti-Christ conquers using talk. Daniel 11 describes the anti-Christ coming in "peaceably," and "obtaining the kingdom by flatteries." So, peace-making diplomacy is another means by which the anti-Christ gains power and world dominion. Then the anti-Christ "devours and brakes in pieces and stamped the residue," (or the rest of the other beasts.) He defeats and takes dominion over the other world powers, taking on the attributes of those he has conquered.

Revelation 13:2 describes the anti-Christ's kingdom after he has annexed and absorbed the three other world powers (beasts): "And the beast which I saw was like unto a leopard (or "tiger"), and his feet were as the feet of a bear, and his mouth as the mouth of a lion: and the dragon gave him his power, and his seat, and great authority." Notice the fourth beast has acquired the other three beasts (world powers) characteristics after subduing them. At the onset of the 7-year tribulation the anti-Christ begins conquering the nations. After 3 1/2 years, he has dominated the world powers.[123]

The ten horns of Daniel 7 correspond to the ten horns of Rev. 13 and to the ten toes described in Daniel 2. Rev. 17:12 states: "And the ten horns which thou saw are ten kings." These nations of the EU power base will unite wholeheartedly behind the anti-Christ (Rev. 17:13.)

Verse 7:8 of Daniel says, *"I considered the horns, and, behold, there came up among them another little horn, before whom there were three of the first horns plucked up by the roots: and, behold, in*

---

this horn were eyes like the eyes of man, and a mouth speaking great things." The "*little horn*" refers to the anti-Christ. Three of the first 10 horns are "plucked up by the roots." This means the rulers of 3 nations are disposed of by the anti-Christ. (Rev. 12:3 shows in the heavenly realm there are 10 horns [countries/sphere of power] with only seven crowns--leaders.) The three crownless horns are 3 countries with no leaders because the anti-Christ supplants them.

The "eyes of a man" mentioned could refer to the all-seeing eye of mystic and occult religion. The "eye" symbolizes knowledge and vision of the spiritual world. This infers the anti-Christ has ties with satanic and occult practices. Daniel 8:23, Revelation 13:4, and II Thes. 2:9 all confirm satanic, deceiving powers at work through the anti-Christ.

Daniel 7:9 describes the anti-Christ conquering nations with "nails of brass." The "brass" is reminiscent of the description of the Greek Empire of Daniel 2. The implication here is that the anti-Christ uses some of the same techniques that Alexander the Great used to expand and control his world empire.

According to World Book (1988 ed., vol.1, pp. 346, 347) Alexander encouraged unity between the nations conquered, including the unity of ideas, customs and laws. In addition to the obvious unity of the EU, this could also refer to the "one world-one earth-New Age movement" mentality that is so prevalent today. Alexander the Great also incorporated soldiers from each of the nations he conquered into his army. The anti-Christ will also have a multinational army. Our present UN "peace-keeping forces" foreshadows the anti-Christ "peace-keeping" army.

Additionally, Alexander the Great implemented a uniform monetary system. The EU already has that. The anti-Christ will implement one economic system for the entire world, so that one cannot buy or sell without the special identification "mark in the hand or in the forehead." (Rev. 13:16) The "mark of the beast" many believe to be microchip implants used for electronic banking. The world's main banking computer is already in the EU headquarters in Brussels: "B.E.A.S.T." (Brussels Electronic Accounting Surveillance Terminal.)

The microchip implants are already used in humans for positive identity. Many nations in Europe (e.g., Sweden) are already almost cashless. Microchip ID is becoming a necessity in order to buy or sell in many places of the world even now.

Lastly, Alexander encouraged the conquered people to worship him as a god. II Thes. 2:3, 4 states: *that man of sin be revealed, the son of perdition; who exalts himself above all that is called God, or that is worshipped; so that he as God sits in the temple of God, showing himself that he is God."*

As Alexander of old, through these techniques the anti-Christ will eventually gain control of the entire world. The anti-Christ's dominion, however, will be short-lived. Daniel 7:9 says that the *"thrones were cast down."* This means that the anti-Christ and the world leaders with him will dethroned and totally defeated.

This defeat occurs when Jesus returns with His saints at the end of the 7-year tribulation to destroy the anti-Christ at Armageddon.[124] Daniel 7:11, 12 describes the anti-Christ thrown into the lake of fire. The other 3 dominions have "their lives prolonged" for a "season" and a "time," possibly corresponding to the short season satan is allowed to tempt the nations before being eternally cast into the lake of fire. Those nations have their dominion taken away, because...

"One like the Son of Man came with the clouds of heaven, and came to the Ancient of Days, and they brought Him near before Him. And there was given Him dominion and glory and a kingdom,

---

[124] Revelation 19:11-21

that all peoples, nations, and languages should serve Him. His dominion is an everlasting dominion, which shall not pass away, and His Kingdom that which shall not be destroyed."

Jesus will take His rightful dominion over all the earth and will rule and reign forever. A m e n ! *Even so, come Lord Jesus!*

IN CONCLUSION

In Conclusion...

God has gone to great lengths to give you the truth about what the Bible predicts will happen to our world. He interrupted a little girl's tetherball game over fifty years ago, gave her a divine vision of the end of the world, mandated that she study Bible prophecy her entire adult life, and share it with you today. God wants you to know that He loves you, no matter what religious affiliation you may have...no matter what sin you may have committed. There is great judgment coming upon the earth. Those who have repented from their sin and asked Jesus to be Lord of their lives will escape that horrible time. I pray that you will be one of them. —Ann

SCRIPTURE REFERENCES AND NOTES:

Acts 7:59-8:1 And they stoned Stephen, calling upon God, and saying, Lord Jesus, receive my spirit. And he kneeled down, and cried with a loud voice, Lord, lay not this sin to their charge. And when he had said this, he fell **asleep.** And Saul was consenting unto his **death.** *[Euphemism for "death" is "sleep" when referring to believers, as it is only a temporary condition from which they will "wake" at the resurrection.]*

Acts 9:1-5 And Saul, yet breathing out threatenings and slaughter **against the disciples** of the Lord, went unto the high priest, 2 and desired of him letters to Damascus to the synagogues, that if he found any of this way, whether they were men or women, he might bring them bound unto Jerusalem. 3 And as he journeyed, he came near Damascus: and suddenly there shined round about him a light from heaven: 4 and he fell to the earth, and heard a voice saying unto him, **Saul, Saul, why persecute thou me**? 5 And he said, Who art thou, Lord? And the Lord said, **I am Jesus whom thou persecute:** *[Christ so closely relates to His Body on earth that He refers to the persecution of believers as persecuting Him.]*

Colossians 3:5, 6-Mortify therefore your members which are upon the earth; fornication, uncleanness, inordinate affection, evil concupiscence, and covetousness, which is idolatry: For which things' sake **the wrath of God cometh on the children of disobedience**: *[God's wrath is never poured out upon His children- it is reserved for the ungodly... the unregenerate.]*

Daniel 2:37-Thou, O king, art a king of kings: for the God of heaven hath given thee a kingdom, power, and strength, and glory. [38] And wheresoever the children of men dwell, the beasts of the field and the fowls of the heaven hath he given into thine hand, and hath made thee ruler over them all. Thou art this head of gold. [39] And after thee shall arise another kingdom inferior to thee, and another third kingdom of brass, which shall bear rule over all the earth. [40] *[Rome was known for its hard military might—iron being an appropriate symbol to describe that empire.]* And the fourth kingdom shall be strong as iron:

116

forasmuch as iron breaks in pieces and subdues all things: and as iron that breaks all these, shall it break in pieces and bruise. [41] And whereas thou saw the feet and toes, part of potters' clay, and part of iron, the kingdom shall be divided; but there shall be in it of the strength of the iron, forasmuch as thou saw the iron mixed with miry clay. [42] And as the toes of the feet were part of iron, and part of clay, so the kingdom shall be partly strong, and partly broken. [43] And whereas thou saw iron mixed with miry clay, they shall mingle themselves with the seed of men: but they shall not cleave one to another, even as iron is not mixed with clay. [44] And in the days of these kings shall the God of heaven set up a kingdom, which shall never be destroyed: and the kingdom shall not be left to other people, but it shall break in pieces and consume all these kingdoms, and it shall stand for ever. *[Gold symbolized the Babylonian empire; silver the Medes-Persian Empire; brass the Grecian empire; iron the Roman Empire. The Roman Empire will re-emerge in the last days as a loose confederacy within the bounds of the old Holy Roman Empire—Europe. The clay/iron not mingling indicates that the individual members of the revived Roman Empire (European Union) maintain some autonomy, but are unified--such as the common currency, shared military, and shared political power.]*

Daniel 7:2-25-Daniel spoke and said, I saw in my vision by night, and, behold, the four winds of the heaven strove upon the great sea. *[These are not a repeat of the 4 historic empires of chapter 2, but rather 4 spheres of power in the last days that are all concurrent with the antichrist kingdom. He actually takes over these powers in his quest for world dominion. The Lion with eagle's wings symbolizes the Western European nations that founded New World-England, Spain. The Eagle's wings refers to the United States. The bear is Russia and its allies. The leopard refers to the Asian powers- i.e. Pacific Rim entities. The 4th beast is the antichrist beast that takes over the other world powers. They all exist concurrently-see Daniel study.]* [3] And four great beasts came up from the sea, di- verse one from another. [4] The first was like a lion, and had eagle's wings: I beheld till the wings thereof were plucked, and it was lifted up from the earth, and made stand upon the feet as a man, and a man's heart was given to it. [5] And behold another beast, a second, like to a bear, and it raised up itself on one side, and it had three ribs in the mouth of it between the teeth of it: and they said thus unto it, Arise, devour much flesh. [6] After this I beheld, and lo another, like a leopard, which had upon the back of it four wings of a fowl; the beast had also four heads; and dominion was given to it. [7] After this I saw in the night visions, and behold a fourth beast, dreadful and terrible, and strong exceedingly; and it had great iron teeth: it devoured and brake in pieces, and stamped the residue with the feet of it: and it was diverse from all the beasts that were before it; and it had ten horns. [8] I considered the horns, and, behold, there came up among them another little horn, before whom there were three of the first horns plucked up by the roots: and, behold, in this horn were eyes like the eyes of man, and a mouth speaking great things. [9] I beheld till the thrones were cast down, and the Ancient of days did sit, whose garment was white as snow, and the hair of his head like the pure wool: his throne was like the fiery flame, and his wheels as burning fire...[19] Then I would know the truth of the fourth beast, which was diverse from all the others, exceeding dreadful, whose teeth were of iron, and his nails of brass; which devoured, brake in pieces, and stamped the residue with his feet; [20] And of the ten horns that were in his head, and of the other which came up, and before whom three fell; even of that horn that had eyes, and a mouth that spoke very great things, whose look was more stout *[antichrist]* than his fellows. [21] I beheld, and the same horn made war with the saints, and prevailed against them; [22] Until the Ancient of days came, and judgment was given to the saints of the most High; and the time came that the saints possessed the kingdom. [23] Thus he said, the fourth beast shall be the fourth kingdom upon earth, which shall be diverse from all kingdoms, and shall devour the whole earth, and shall tread it down, and break it in pieces. [24] And the ten horns out of this kingdom are ten kings that shall arise: and another shall rise after them; and he shall be diverse from the first, and he shall subdue three kings. [25] And he shall speak great words against the most High, and shall wear out the saints of the most High, and think to change times and laws: and they shall be given into his hand until a time and times and the dividing of time.

Daniel 8: Therefore the he goat waxed very great: and when he was strong, the great horn was broken; and for it came up four notable ones toward the four winds of heaven. 9 And out of one of them came forth a little horn, which waxed exceeding great, toward the south, and toward the east, and toward the pleasant land. 10 And it waxed great, even to the host of heaven; and it cast down some of the host and of the stars to the ground, and stamped upon them. 11 Yea, he magnified himself even to the prince of the host, and by him the daily sacrifice was taken away, and the place of his sanctuary was cast down. 12 And an host was given him against the daily sacrifice by reason of transgression, and it cast down the truth to the ground; and it practiced, and prospered.

[Antiochus Epiphanes is referred to here, though he foreshadows the antichrist by defiling the Temple. The Maccabees had this prophecy written several hundred years before the fact to trust in, knowing that God would give them victory when they took back the temple and rededicated it exactly as Daniel predicted here— after 2,300 days.] 13 Then I heard one saint speaking, and another saint said unto that certain saint which spoke, How long shall be the vision concerning the daily sacrifice, and the transgression of desolation, to give both the sanctuary and the host to be trodden under foot? 14 And he said unto me, Unto two thousand and three hundred days; then shall the sanctuary be cleansed.

Daniel 9:24-27 Seventy weeks are determined upon thy people and upon thy holy city, to finish the transgression, and to make an end of sins, and to make reconciliation for iniquity, and to bring in everlasting righteousness, and to seal up the vision and prophecy, and to anoint the most Holy. 25 Know therefore and understand, that from the going forth of the commandment to restore and to build Jerusalem unto the Messiah the Prince shall be seven weeks, and threescore and two weeks: the street shall be built again, and the wall, even in troublous times. *[The decree to rebuild the street and the walls was given by Artaxerxes Longimanus in 445 B.C. The 62 "weeks" – periods of seven years- ended in 31 A.D. when most scholars believe Jesus Messiah was crucified.]* 26 And after threescore and two weeks shall **Messiah be cut off, but not for himself**: and the people of the prince that shall come shall **destroy**

the city and the sanctuary; and the end thereof shall be with a flood, and unto the end of the war desolations are determined. 27 And he shall confirm the covenant with many for one week: and in the midst of the week he shall cause the sacrifice and the oblation to cease, and for the overspreading of abominations he shall make it desolate, even until the consummation, and that determined shall be poured upon the desolate. *[The exact time when Messiah would be cut off in the first century was predicted by Daniel almost 500 years in advance, while also predicting the Temple's destruction that followed in 70 A.D. by General Titus.]*

Daniel 11 Also I in the first year of Darius the **Mede**, even I, stood to confirm and to strengthen him. And now will I show thee the truth. Behold, there shall stand up yet three kings in **Persia**; and the fourth shall be far richer than they all: and by his strength through his riches he shall stir up all against the realm of **Grecia.** And a mighty king shall stand up, that shall rule with great dominion, and do according to his will. And a mighty king shall stand up, that shall rule with great dominion, and do according to his will. [4] And when **he** shall stand up **his kingdom shall be broken, and shall be divided toward the four winds of heaven; and not to his posterity**, *[Alexander the Great and his four generals who took over after his death]* nor according to his dominion which he ruled: for his kingdom shall be plucked up, even for others beside those. [5] *[King of South= Egypt Ptolemies kingdom; King of North=Seleucids of Syria]* And the king of the south shall be strong, and one of his princes; and he shall be strong above him, and have dominion; his dominion shall be a great dominion. And in the end of years they shall join themselves together; for the **king's daughter of the south** shall come to the king of the north to make an agreement: but she shall not retain the power of the arm; neither shall he stand, nor his arm: but she shall be given up, and they that brought her, and he that begat her, and he that strengthened her in these times. But out of a branch of her roots shall one stand up in his estate, which shall come with an army, and shall enter into the fortress of the king of the north, and shall deal against them, and shall prevail...

Daniel 11:36 *[the text transitions into the antichrist end-times prophecy at this verse]* And the king shall do according to his will; and he shall exalt himself, and magnify himself above every god, and shall speak marvelous things against the God of gods, and shall prosper till the indignation be accomplished: for that that is determined shall be done. 37 Neither shall he regard the God of his fathers, nor the desire of women, nor regard any god: for he shall magnify himself above all. 38 But in his estate shall he honor the God of forces: and a god whom his fathers knew not shall he honor with gold, and silver, and with precious stones, and pleasant things. 39 Thus shall he do in the most strong holds with a strange god, whom he shall acknowledge and increase with glory: and he shall cause them to rule over many, and shall divide the land for gain.40 And at the time of the end shall the king of the south push at him: and the king of the north shall come against him like a whirlwind, with chariots, and with horsemen, and with many ships; and he shall enter into the countries, and shall overflow and pass over. 41 He shall enter also into the glorious land, and many countries shall be overthrown: but these shall escape out of his hand, even Edom, and Moab, and the chief of the children of Ammon.-*[Parts of Syria and Jordan seem to escape antichrist dominion—perhaps they are rendered desolate by previous wars such as Psalm 83 regional war with Israel.]* 42 He shall stretch forth his hand also upon the countries: and the land of Egypt shall not escape. 43 But he shall have power over the treasures of gold and of silver, and over all the precious things of Egypt: and the Libyans and the Ethiopians shall be at his steps. 44 But tidings out of the east and out of the north shall trouble him: therefore he shall go forth with great fury to destroy, and utterly to make away many. 45 And he shall plant the tabernacles of his palace between the seas in the glorious holy mountain; yet he shall come to his end, and none shall help him. *[Antichrist and his invasion of Israel]*

Exodus 7:20- And Moses and Aaron did so, as the LORD commanded; and he lifted up the rod, and smote the waters that were in the river, in the sight of Pharaoh, and in the sight of his servants; and all the waters that were in the river were turned to blood. [21] And the fish that was in the river died; and the river stank, and the

Egyptians could not drink of the water of the river; and there was blood throughout all the land of Egypt. [22] **And the magicians of Egypt <u>did so with their enchantments</u>**: and Pharaoh's heart was hardened, neither did he hearken unto them; as the LORD had said.

Ezekiel 4:[1] Thou also, son of man, take thee a tile, and lay it before thee, and portray upon it the city, even Jerusalem: [2] And lay siege against it, and build a fort against it, and cast a mount against it; set the camp also against it, and set battering rams against it round about. [3] Moreover take thou unto thee an iron pan, and set it for a wall of iron between thee and the city: and set thy face against it, and it shall be besieged, and thou shalt lay siege against it. This shall be a sign to the house of Israel. [4] Lie thou also upon thy left side, and lay the iniquity of the house of Israel upon it: according to the number of the days that thou shalt lie upon it thou shalt bear their iniquity. [5] For I have laid upon thee **the years of their iniquity, according to the number of the days, three hundred and ninety days**: so shalt thou bear the iniquity of the house of Israel. [6] And when thou hast accomplished them, lie again on thy right side, and thou shalt bear the iniquity of the house of Judah **forty days: I have appointed thee each day for a year**. [7] Therefore thou shalt set thy face toward the siege of Jerusalem, and thine arm shall be uncovered, and thou shalt prophesy against it. [8] And, behold, I will lay bands upon thee, and thou shalt not turn thee from one side to another, till thou hast ended the days of thy siege. [9] Take thou also unto thee wheat, and barley, and beans, and lentils, and millet, and fitches, and put them in one vessel, and make thee bread thereof, according to the number of the days that thou shalt lie upon thy side, three hundred and ninety days shalt thou eat thereof. [10] And thy meat which thou shalt eat shall be by weight, twenty shekels a day: from time to time shalt thou eat it. [11] Thou shalt drink also water by measure, the sixth part of an hin: from time to time shalt thou drink. [12] And thou shalt eat it as barley cakes, and thou shalt bake it with dung that cometh out of man, in their sight. [13] And the LORD said, Even thus shall the children of Israel eat their defiled bread among the Gentiles, whither I will drive them.

Ezekiel 38:8 After many days thou shalt be visited: in **the latter years** thou shalt come into the land that is brought back from the sword, *[Israel after the WWII Holocaust]* and is gathered out of many people, against the mountains of Israel, which have been always waste: but it is brought forth out of the nations, and they shall dwell safely all of them.

Genesis 6:2, 5, 11-that the sons of God saw the daughters of men that they were fair; and they took them wives of all which they chose. 5 And God saw that the **wickedness of man was great** in the earth, and that **every imagination of the thoughts of his heart was only evil continually**. 11 The earth also was **corrupt** before God, and the earth was **filled with violence.**

Genesis 7:11,24 8:4- In the six hundredth year of Noah's life, in the **second month, the seventeenth day of the month**, the same day were all the fountains of the great deep broken up, and the windows of heaven were opened. And the waters prevailed upon the earth an **hundred and fifty days**. And the waters returned from off the earth continually: and after the end of the hundred and fifty days the waters were abated. And the ark rested in the **seventh *month*, on the seventeenth day of the month**, upon the mountains of Ararat. *[Biblical months are 30 days, a Biblical year is 360 days—lunar calendar. The five months that transpired here was exactly 150 days-five months]*

Genesis 37:9 And he dreamed yet another dream, and told it his brethren, and said, Behold, I have dreamed a dream more; and, behold, the **sun and the moon and the eleven stars** made obeisance to me. 10 And he told it to his father, and to his brethren: and his father rebuked him, and said unto him *[Jacob, his wife, and children depicted as celestial bodies—corresponds to book of Revelation symbol of Israel during the Great Tribulation time]* What is this dream that thou hast dreamed? Shall **I and thy mother and thy brethren** indeed come to bow down ourselves to thee to the earth?

Hebrews 3:7-11-To day if ye will hear his voice, 8 harden not your hearts, as in the provocation, in the day of temptation in the wilderness: 9 when your fathers tempted me, proved me, and saw my works forty years. 10 Wherefore **I was grieved with that generation**, and said, They do alway err in their heart; and they have not known my ways. 11 So I swore in my wrath, They shall not enter into my rest.) *[The "generation" that grieved God were those 20 years old and over who died in the wilderness.]*

Hebrews 9:27 And as it is appointed unto men once to die, but after this the judgment: 28 so Christ was once offered to bear the sins of many; and **unto them that look for Him shall He appear the second time without sin unto salvation.** *[When Christ comes for the Church at the Rapture only to the Church will He appear. When He returns to earth at the end of the seven-year tribulation "every eye" will see Him.]*

Hosea 11:1-11 When Israel was a child, then I loved him, and **called My son out of Egypt.**

I Corinthians 2:9-But as it is written, Eye hath not seen, nor ear heard, neither have entered into the heart of man, the things which God hath prepared for them that love him.

I Thessalonians 1:10- how ye turned to God from idols to serve the living and true God; 10 **And to wait for his Son from heaven,** whom he raised from the dead, *even Jesus, which delivered us from the wrath to come.*

I Timothy 2:5-For there is one God, and one mediator between God and men, the man Christ Jesus; 6 who gave himself a ransom for all, to be testified in due time.

II Corinthians 11:2-4 For I am jealous over you with godly jealousy: for I have espoused you to one husband, that I may present you as a **chaste virgin to Christ**. But I fear, lest by any means, as the serpent beguiled Eve through his subtlety, so your minds should be corrupted from the simplicity that is in Christ. [4] For if he that cometh preaches another Jesus, whom we have not preached, or if **ye receive another spirit**, which ye have not received, or another gospel, which ye have not accepted, ye might well bear with him.

II John [7] For many deceivers are entered into the world, who **confess not that Jesus Christ is come in the flesh.** This is a deceiver and an antichrist. [8] Look to yourselves, that we lose not those things which we have wrought, but that we receive a full reward. [9] Whosoever transgresses, and abides not in the doctrine of Christ, hath not God. He that abides in the doctrine of Christ, he hath both the Father and the Son. [10] If there come any unto you, and bring not this doctrine, receive him not into your house, neither bid him God speed: [11] For he that bids him God speed is partaker of his evil deeds.

II Peter 1:10 Wherefore the rather, brethren, give diligence to make your calling and election sure: for if ye do these things, ye shall never fall: 11 for so **an entrance** shall be ministered unto you abundantly into the everlasting kingdom of our Lord and Savior Jesus Christ.

II Peter 1:21-For the **prophecy came not in old time by the will of man: but holy men of God spoke as they were moved by the Holy Ghost**.

II Thessalonians 1:4-10- So that we ourselves glory in you in the churches of God for your patience and faith in all your persecutions and tribulations that ye endure: 5 which is a manifest token of the righteous judgment of God, that ye may be counted worthy of the kingdom of God, for which ye also suffer: 6 seeing **it is a righteous thing with God to recompense tribulation to them that trouble you; 7 and to you who are troubled rest with us, when the Lord Jesus shall be revealed from heaven with his mighty angels**, 8 in flaming fire taking vengeance on them that know not God, and that obey not the gospel of our Lord Jesus Christ: 9 who shall be punished with everlasting destruction from the presence of the Lord, and from the glory of his power; 10 when he shall come to be glorified in his saints, and to be admired in all them that believe (because our testimony among you was believed) in that day.

II Thessalonians 2:3- Let no man deceive you by any means: **for that day shall not come, except there come a falling away first, and that man of sin be revealed, the son of perdition**; 4 who opposes and exalts himself above all that is called God, or that is worshipped; so that he as God sits in the temple of God, showing himself that he is God.

II Timothy 3:16-16 All scripture is given by inspiration of God, and is profitable for doctrine, for reproof, for correction, for instruction in righteousness: That the man of God may be perfect, thoroughly furnished unto all good works.

II Timothy 4:10- For **Demas hath forsaken me**, having loved this present world, and is **departed** unto Thessalonica...

Isaiah 7:14 Therefore the Lord himself shall give you a sign; Behold, **a virgin shall conceive, and bear a son, and shall call his name Immanuel. 15 Butter and honey shall he eat, that he may know to refuse the evil, and choose the good. 16 For before the child shall know to refuse the evil, and choose the good, the land that thou abhor shall be forsaken of both her kings.**17 The Lord shall bring upon thee, and upon thy people, and upon thy father's house, days that have not come, from the day that Ephraim departed from Judah; even the king of Assyria.

Isaiah 8:3 And I went unto the prophetess; and **she conceived, and bare a son.** Then said the Lord to me, Call his name Maher-shalal-hash-baz. 4 **For before the child shall have knowledge to cry, My father, and my mother,** the riches of Damascus and the spoil of Samaria shall be taken away **before the king of Assyria.**

Isaiah 9:1,2-9 Nevertheless the dimness shall not be such as was in her vexation, when at the first he lightly afflicted the land of Zebulun and the land of Naphtali, and afterward did more grievously afflict her by the way of the sea, beyond Jordan, in **Galilee** of the nations. 2 The people that walked in darkness have seen a **great light**: they that dwell in the land of the shadow of death, upon them hath the light shined.

Isaiah 16:1-Send ye the lamb to the ruler of the land **from Sela to the wilderness**, unto the mount of the daughter of Zion.2 For it shall be, that, as a wandering bird cast out of the nest, so the daughters of Moab shall be at the fords of Arnon.3 Take counsel, execute judgment; make thy shadow as the night in the midst of the noonday; hide the outcasts; betray not him that wandereth. 4 **Let mine outcasts dwell with thee, Moab; be thou a covert to them from the face of the spoiler:** for the extortioner is at an end, the spoiler ceases, the oppressors are consumed out of the land.

Isa.18- [1] Woe to the **land shadowing with wings**, which is beyond the rivers of Ethiopia: [2] That sends **ambassadors by the sea**, even in vessels of bulrushes upon the waters, saying, Go, ye swift messengers, to a nation scattered and peeled, to a people terrible from their beginning hitherto; a nation meted out and trodden down, whose land the rivers have spoiled! [3] All ye inhabitants of the world, and dwellers on the earth, see ye, when he lifts up an ensign on the mountains; and when he blows a trumpet, hear ye. [4] For so the LORD said unto me, I will take my rest, and I will consider in my dwelling place like a clear heat upon herbs, and like a cloud of dew in the heat of harvest. [5] For afore the harvest, when the bud is perfect, and the sour grape is ripening in the flower, he shall both cut off the sprigs with pruning hooks, and take away and cut down the branches. [6] They shall be left together unto the fowls of the mountains, and to the beasts of the earth: and the fowls shall summer upon them, and all the beasts of the earth shall winter upon them. [7] In that time shall the present be brought unto the LORD of hosts of a people scattered and peeled, and from a people terrible from their beginning hitherto; a nation meted out and trodden under foot, whose land the rivers have spoiled, to the place of the name of the LORD of hosts, the mount Zion. [Allusion to national emblem of outstretched eagle's wings can imply the U.S.]

Isaiah 35:1, 2-The wilderness and the solitary place shall be glad for them; and the **desert shall rejoice, and blossom as the rose.** 2 It shall blossom abundantly, and rejoice even with joy and singing: the glory of Lebanon shall be given unto it, the excellency of Carmel and Sharon, they shall see the glory of the Lord, and the excellency of our God.

Isaiah 44:28-That says of **Cyrus**, He is my shepherd, and shall perform all my pleasure: even saying to **Jerusalem, Thou shalt be built; and to the temple, Thy foundation shall be laid.**

Isa.47:[1] Come down, and sit in the dust, O virgin **daughter of Babylon**, sit on the ground: there is no throne, O daughter of the Chaldeans: for thou shalt no more be called tender and delicate. [2] Take the millstones, and grind meal: uncover thy locks, make bare the leg, uncover the thigh, pass over the rivers. [3] Thy nakedness shall be uncovered, yea, thy shame shall be seen: I will take vengeance, and I will not meet thee as a man. [4] As for our redeemer, the LORD of hosts is his name, the Holy One of Israel. [5] Sit thou silent, and get thee into darkness, **O daughter of the Chaldeans: for thou shalt no more be called, The lady of kingdoms. [6] I was wroth with my people, I have polluted mine inheritance, and given them into thine hand: thou didst shew them no mercy; upon the ancient hast thou very heavily laid thy yoke. [7] And thou said, I shall be a lady forever: so that thou didst not lay these things to thy heart, neither didst remember the latter end of it. [8] Therefore hear now this, thou that art given to pleasures, that dwell carelessly, that say in thine heart, I am, and none else beside me; I shall not sit as a widow, neither shall I know the loss of children: [9] But these two things shall come to thee in a moment in one day, the loss of children, and widowhood**: they shall come upon thee in their perfection for the multitude of thy sorceries, and for the great abundance of thine enchantments. [10] For thou hast trusted in thy wickedness: thou hast said, None sees me. Thy wisdom and thy knowledge, it hath perverted thee; and thou hast said in thine heart, I am, and none else beside me. [11] **Therefore shall evil come upon thee; thou shalt not know from whence it rises: and mischief shall fall upon thee; thou shalt not be able to put it off: and desolation shall come upon thee suddenly, which thou shalt not know**. [12] Stand now with thine enchantments, and with the multitude of thy sorceries, wherein thou hast labored from thy youth; if so be thou shalt be able to profit, if so be thou may prevail. [13] Thou art wearied in the multitude of thy counsels. Let now the astrologers, the stargazers, the monthly prognosticators, stand up, and save thee from these things that shall come upon thee. [14] Behold, they shall be as stubble; the fire shall burn them; they shall not deliver themselves from the power of the flame: there shall not be a coal to warm at, nor fire to sit before it. [15] Thus shall they be unto thee with whom thou hast labored, even thy merchants, from thy youth: they shall wander everyone to his quarter; none shall save thee.

Isaiah 53: Who hath believed our report? and to whom is the arm of the LORD revealed? For he shall grow up before him as a tender plant, and as a root out of a dry ground: he hath no form nor comeliness; and when we shall see him, there is no beauty that we should desire him. He is **despised and rejected of men**; a man of sorrows, and acquainted with grief: and we hid as it were our faces from him; **he was despised, and we esteemed him not**. Surely he hath borne our **griefs, and carried our sorrows**: yet we did esteem him stricken, smitten of God, and afflicted. But he was wounded for our transgressions, he was bruised for our iniquities: **the chastisement of our peace was upon him; and with his stripes we are healed**. All we like sheep have gone astray; we have turned everyone to his own way; and the **LORD hath laid on him the iniquity of us all**.] He was oppressed, and he was afflicted, yet he opened not his mouth: he is brought as a lamb to the slaughter, and as a **sheep before her shearers is dumb, so he opens not his mouth**. He was **taken from prison and from judgment: and who shall declare his generation? for he was cut off out of the land of the living:** for the transgression of my people was he stricken. And he made his **grave with the wicked**, and with the **rich in his death**; because he had done no violence, neither was any deceit in his mouth. Yet it pleased the LORD to bruise him; he hath put him to grief: when thou shalt make his soul an offering for sin, he shall see his seed, he shall prolong his days, and the pleasure of the LORD shall prosper in his hand. He shall see of the travail of his soul, and shall be satisfied: by his knowledge shall my righteous servant justify many; for he shall bear their iniquities.] Therefore, will I divide him a portion with the great, and he shall divide the spoil with the strong; because **he hath poured out his soul unto death: and he was numbered with the transgressors; and he bare the sin of many, and made intercession for the transgressors.**

James 1:18: "Of His own will begat He us with the Word of Truth, that we should be a kind of **firstfruits** of His creatures."

Jeremiah 23:10-For **the land is full of adulterers**; for because of swearing the land mourns; the pleasant places of **the wilderness are dried up**, and their course is evil, and their force is not right. 11 For both **prophet and priest are profane**; yea, in my house have I found their wickedness, says the Lord. 12 Wherefore their way shall be unto them as slippery ways in the darkness: they shall be driven on, and fall herein: for I will bring evil upon them, even the year of their visitation, says the Lord. 13 And I have seen folly in the prophets of Samaria; they prophesied in Baal, and caused my people Israel to err. 14 I have seen also in the prophets of Jerusalem an horrible thing: **they commit adultery, and walk in lies**: they strengthen also the hands of evildoers, that none doth return from his wickedness: they are all of them unto me as Sodom, and the inhabitants thereof as Gomorrah. 15 Therefore thus says the Lord of hosts concerning the prophets; Behold, I will feed them with wormwood, and make them drink the water of gall: for from the prophets of Jerusalem is profaneness gone forth into all the land. 16 Thus says the Lord of hosts, Hearken not unto the words of the prophets that prophesy unto you: they make you vain: they speak a vision of their own heart, and not out of the mouth of the Lord. 17 They say still unto them that despise me, The Lord hath said, **You shall have peace; and they say unto every one that walks after the**

imagination of his own heart, No evil shall come upon you. [*Typical of the "feel good" false, hyper-grace teaching that one can live like the devil and still make heaven.*]18 For who hath stood in the counsel of the Lord, and hath perceived and heard his word? who hath marked his word, and heard it? 19 Behold, **a whirlwind of the Lord is gone forth in fury, even a grievous whirlwind:** it shall fall grievously upon the head of the wicked. 20 The anger of the Lord shall not return, until he have executed, and till he have performed the thoughts of his heart: **in the latter days** ye shall consider it perfectly.

Jeremiah 30:7- Alas! for that day is great, so that none is like it: it is even the time of **Jacob's trouble**; but he shall be ___saved out of it___ [*literally to be fulfilled when the 144,000 are raptured in the middle of the tribulation as Daniel 12, Revelation 12 & 14 depict.*]

Jeremiah 44-And I will take the remnant of Judah, that have set their faces to go into the land of Egypt to sojourn there, and they shall all be consumed, and fall in the land of Egypt; they shall even be consumed by the sword and by the famine: they shall die, from the least even unto the greatest, by the sword and by the famine: and they shall be an execration, and an astonishment, and a curse, and a reproach. 13 For I will punish them that dwell in the land of Egypt, as I have punished Jerusalem, by the sword, by the famine, and by the pestilence: 14 so that none of the remnant of Judah, which are gone into the land of Egypt to sojourn there, shall escape or remain, that they should return into the land of Judah, to the which they have a desire to return to dwell there: for none shall return but such as shall escape.15 **Then all the men which knew that their wives had burned incense unto other gods, and all the women that stood by, a great multitude, even all the people that dwelt in the land of Egypt, in Pathros, answered Jeremiah, saying, 16 As for the word that thou hast spoken unto us in the name of the Lord, we will not hearken unto thee.** 17 But we will certainly do whatsoever thing goes forth out of our own mouth, to burn incense unto **the queen of heaven,** and to pour out drink offerings unto her, as we have done, we, and our fathers, our kings, and our princes, in the cities of Judah.

Jeremiah 50:1-The word that the LORD spake against Babylon and against the land of the Chaldeans by Jeremiah the prophet. [2] Declare ye among the nations, and publish, and set up a standard; publish, and conceal not: say, Babylon is taken, Bel is confounded, Merodach is broken in pieces; her idols are confounded, her images are broken in pieces.**[3] For out of the north there cometh up a nation against her, which shall make her land desolate, and none shall dwell therein: they shall remove, they shall depart, both man and beast. [4] In those days, and in that time, saith the LORD, the children of Israel shall come, they and the children of Judah together, going and weeping: they shall go, and seek the LORD their God.[5] They shall ask the way to Zion with their faces thitherward, saying, Come, and let us join ourselves to the LORD in a perpetual covenant that shall not be forgotten.[6] My people hath been lost sheep: their shepherds have caused them to go astray, they have turned them away on the mountains: they have gone from mountain to hill, they have forgotten their resting place. [7] All that found them have devoured them: and their adversaries said, We offend not, because they have sinned against the LORD, the habitation of justice, even the LORD, the hope of their fathers. [8] Remove out of the midst of Babylon, and go forth out of the land of the Chaldeans, and be as the he goats before the flocks. [9] For, lo, I will raise and cause to come up against Babylon an assembly of great nations from the north country: and they shall set themselves in array against her; from thence she shall be taken: their arrows shall be as of a mighty expert man; none shall return in vain.[10] And Chaldea shall be a spoil: all that spoil her shall be satisfied, saith the LORD.[11] Because ye were glad, because ye rejoiced, O ye destroyers of mine heritage, because ye are grown fat as the heifer at grass, and bellow as bulls;[12] Your mother shall be sore confounded; she that bare you shall be ashamed: behold, the hindermost of the nations shall be a wilderness, a dry land, and a desert. [13] Because of the wrath of the LORD it shall not be inhabited, but it shall be wholly desolate: every one that goeth by Babylon shall**

be astonished, and hiss at all her plagues. **[14] Put yourselves in array against Babylon round about: all ye that bend the bow, shoot at her, spare no arrows: for she hath sinned against the LORD.**[15] Shout against her round about: she hath given her hand: her foundations are fallen, her walls are thrown down: for it is the vengeance of the LORD: take vengeance upon her; as she hath done, do unto her.[16] Cut off the sower from Babylon, and him that handleth the sickle in the time of harvest: for fear of the oppressing sword they shall turn every one to his people, and they shall flee every one to his own land, Call together the archers against Babylon: all ye that bend the bow, camp against it round about; let none thereof escape: recompense her according to her work; according to all that she hath done, do unto her: **for she hath been proud against the LORD**, against the Holy One of Israel. [30] Therefore shall her young men fall in the streets, and all her men of war shall be cut off in that day, saith the LORD. [31] Behold, I am against thee, O thou most proud, saith the Lord GOD of hosts: for thy day is come, the time that I will visit thee.[32] And the most proud shall stumble and fall, and none shall raise him up: and I will kindle a fire in his cities, and it shall devour all round about him.

Jer.51:[1] Thus saith the LORD; Behold, I will raise up against Babylon, and against them that dwell in the midst of them that rise up against me, a destroying wind;[2] And will send unto Babylon fanners, that shall fan her, and shall empty her land: for in the day of trouble they shall be against her round about. [3] Against him that bendeth let the archer bend his bow, and against him that lifteth himself up in his brigandine: and spare ye not her young men; destroy ye utterly all her host.[4] Thus the slain shall fall in the land of the Chaldeans, and they that are thrust through in her streets. [5] For Israel hath not been forsaken, nor Judah of his God, of the LORD of hosts; though their land was filled with sin against the Holy One of Israel. **[6] Flee out of the midst of Babylon, and deliver every man his soul: be not cut off in her iniquity; for this is the time of the LORD's vengeance; he will render unto her a recompence. [7] Babylon hath been a golden cup in the LORD's hand, that made all the earth drunken: the**

nations have drunken of her wine; therefore the nations are mad. **[8] Babylon is suddenly fallen and destroyed: howl for her; take balm for her pain, if so she may be healed. [9] We would have healed Babylon, but she is not healed: forsake her, and let us go every one into his own country: for her judgment reacheth unto heaven, and is lifted up even to the skies. [10] The LORD hath brought forth our righteousness: come, and let us declare in Zion the work of the LORD our God.** [11] Make bright the arrows; gather the shields: the LORD hath raised up the spirit of the kings of the Medes: for his device is against Babylon, to destroy it; because it is the vengeance of the LORD, the vengeance of his temple. [12] Set up the standard upon the walls of Babylon, make the watch strong, set up the watchmen, prepare the ambushes: for the LORD hath both devised and done that which he spake against the inhabitants of Babylon. [13] **O thou that dwells upon many waters, abundant in treasures, thine end is come, and the measure of thy covetousness.** [14] The LORD of hosts hath sworn by himself, saying, Surely I will fill thee with men, as with caterpillers; and they shall lift up a shout against thee. [15] He hath made the earth by his power, he hath established the world by his wisdom, and hath stretched out the heaven by his under- standing. [16] When he utters his voice, there is a multitude of waters in the heavens; and he causes the vapors to ascend from the ends of the earth: he makes lightnings with rain, and brings forth the wind out of his treasures. [17] Every man is brutish by his knowledge; every founder is confounded by the graven image: for his molten image is falsehood, and there is no breath in them. [18] They are vanity, the work of errors: in the time of their visitation they shall perish. [19] The portion of Jacob is not like them; for he is the former of all things: and Israel is the rod of his inheritance: the LORD of hosts is his name. [20] Thou art my battle axe and weapons of war: for with thee will I break in pieces the nations, and with thee will I destroy kingdoms; [21] And with thee will I break in pieces the horse and his rider; and with thee will I break in pieces the chariot and his rider; [22] With thee also will I break in pieces man and woman; and with thee will I break in pieces old and young; and with thee will I break in pieces the young man and the maid; [23] I will also break in pieces with thee the shepherd and his flock; and with thee will I break in pieces the husbandman and his yoke of oxen; and with thee will I break in pieces captains and rulers. [24] And I will render unto Babylon and to all the inhabitants of Chaldea all their evil that they have done in Zion in your sight, saith the LORD. [25] Behold, I am against thee, **O destroying mountain, saith the LORD, which destroyest all the earth: and I will stretch out mine hand upon thee, and roll thee down from the rocks, and will make thee a burnt mountain. [26] And they shall not take of thee a stone for a corner, nor a stone for foundations; but thou shalt be desolate for ever, saith the LORD. [27] Set ye up a standard in the land, blow the trumpet among the nations, prepare the nations against her, call together against her the kingdoms of Ararat, Minni, and Ashchenaz; appoint a captain against her**; cause the horses to come up as the rough caterpillers. [28] Prepare against her the nations with the kings of the Medes, the captains thereof, and all the rulers thereof, and all the land of his dominion. [29] And **the land shall tremble and sorrow: for every purpose of the LORD shall be performed against Babylon, to make the land of Babylon a desolation without an inhabitant...** [37] And Babylon shall become heaps, a dwellingplace for dragons, an astonishment, and an hissing, without an inhabitant. [38] They shall roar together like lions: they shall **yell as lion's whelps**...The sea is come up upon Babylon: she is covered with the multitude of the waves thereof. [43] Her cities are a desolation, a dry land, and a wilderness, a land wherein no man dwelleth, neither doth any son of man pass thereby.

John 3:3-7- Jesus answered and said unto him, Verily, verily, I say unto thee, **Except a man be born again, he cannot see the kingdom of God.** [4] Nicodemus says unto him, How can a man be born when he is old? can he enter the second time into his mother's womb, and be born? [5] Jesus answered, Verily, verily, I say unto thee, Except a man be born of water and of the Spirit, he cannot enter into the kingdom of God. [6] That which is born of the flesh is flesh; and that which is born of the Spirit is spirit. [7] Marvel not that I said unto thee, Ye must be born again.

John 5:28- Marvel not at this: for the hour is coming, in the which all that are in the graves shall hear his voice, [29] And shall come forth; they that have done good, unto the **resurrection of life;** and they that have done evil, unto the **resurrection of damnation**.

John 14:1-6 Let not your heart be troubled: ye believe in God, believe also in me. 2 In my Father's house are many mansions: if it were not so, I would have told you. I go to prepare a place for you.3 And if **I go and prepare a place for you, I will come again, and receive you unto myself; that where I am, there you may be also.** And whither I go ye know, and the way ye know. Thomas said unto him, Lord, we know not where you are going; and how can we know the way? Jesus said unto him, I am the way, the truth, and the life: no man cometh unto the Father, but by me.

John 16:13, 14-Howbeit when he, **the Spirit of truth, is** come, he will guide you into all truth: for he shall not speak of himself; but whatsoever he shall hear, that shall he speak: and he will show you things to come. [14] **He shall glorify me**: for he shall receive of mine, and shall show it unto you.

Jude 14, 15 And Enoch also, the seventh from Adam, prophesied of these, saying, Behold, **the Lord cometh with ten thousands of his saints**, 15 to execute judgment upon all, and to convince all that are ungodly among them of all their ungodly deeds which they have ungodly committed, and of all their hard speeches which ungodly sinners have spoken against him.

Leviticus 26:15-18- And if ye shall despise my statutes, or if your soul abhor my judgments, so that ye will not do all my commandments, but that ye break my covenant: I also will do this unto you; I will even appoint over you terror, consumption, and the burning ague, that shall consume the eyes, and cause sorrow of heart: and ye shall sow your seed in vain, for your enemies shall eat it. And I will set my face against you, and ye shall be slain before your enemies: **they that hate you shall reign over**

you; and ye shall flee when none pursues you. **And if ye will not yet for all this hearken unto me, then I will punish you seven times more for your sins.**

Luke 2:7-15 And she brought forth **her firstborn son,** and wrapped him in swaddling clothes, and **laid him in a manger;** because there was no room for them in the inn. And there were in the same country shepherds abiding in the field, keeping watch over their flock by night. And, lo, the angel of the Lord came upon them, and the glory of the Lord shone round about them: and they were sore afraid. And the angel said unto them, Fear not: for, behold, I bring you good tidings of great joy, which shall be to all people. **For unto you is born this day in the city of David a Savior, which is Christ the Lord...** And it came to pass, as the angels were gone away from them into heaven, **the shepherds said one to another, Let us now go even unto Bethlehem,** and see this thing which is come to pass, which the Lord hath made known unto us.

Luke 14:14-And thou shalt be blessed; for they cannot recompense thee: for thou shalt be recompensed at **the resurrection of the just**.

Luke 21:5...28 And as some spoke of the temple, how it was adorned with goodly stones and gifts, he said, As for these things which ye behold, the days will come, in the which there shall **not be left one stone upon another**, that shall not be thrown down. And they asked him, saying, Master, but when shall **these things be**? And what sign will there be when these things shall come to pass? ...Then said he unto them, **Nation shall rise against nation, and kingdom against kingdom: And great earthquakes shall be in divers places, and famines, and pestilences; and fearful sights and great signs shall there be from heaven... V. 25-And there shall be signs in the sun, and in the moon, and in the stars; and upon the earth distress of nations, with perplexity; the sea and the waves roaring; Men's hearts failing them for fear, and for looking after those things which are coming on the earth:** for the powers of heaven shall be shaken. And then shall they see the Son of man coming in a cloud with power and great glory. And when these things begin to come to pass, then look up, and lift up your heads; for your redemption draws nigh.

Luke 21:34 And take heed to yourselves, lest at any time your hearts be overcharged with surfeiting, and drunkenness, and cares of this life, and so that day come upon you unawares. 35 For as a snare shall it come on all them that dwell on the face of the whole earth. 36 Watch ye therefore, and pray al- ways, that ye may be accounted worthy to escape all these things that shall come to pass, and to stand before the Son of man.

Luke 24:36- And as they thus spoke, Jesus himself stood in the midst of them, and said unto them, Peace be unto you. But they were terrified and affrighted, and supposed that they had seen a spirit. And he said unto them, Why are ye troubled? and why do thoughts arise in your hearts? Behold my hands and my feet, that it is I myself: handle me, and see; for **a spirit hath not flesh and bones, as ye see me have**. And when he had thus spoken, he showed them his hands and his feet.

Malachi 4:4 For, behold, the day cometh, that shall burn as an oven; and all the proud, yea, and all that do wickedly, shall be stubble: and the day that cometh shall burn them up, says the Lord of hosts, that it shall leave them neither root nor branch. 2 But unto you that fear my name shall the Sun of righteousness arise with healing in his wings; and ye shall go forth, and grow up as calves of the stall. 3 And ye shall tread down the wicked; for they shall be ashes under the soles of your feet in the day that I shall do this, says the Lord of hosts.4 Remember ye the law of Moses my servant, which I commanded unto him in Horeb for all Israel, with the statutes and judgments.5 **Behold, I will send you Elijah the prophet before the coming of the great and dreadful day of the Lord**: 6 and he shall turn the heart of the fathers to the children, and the heart of the children to their fathers, lest I come and smite the earth with a curse.

Mark 13:14- But when ye shall see the **abomination of desolation,** spoken of by Daniel the prophet, standing where it ought not, (let him that reads understand,) then let them that be in Judæa flee to the mountains:

Mark 16:15-And he said unto them, Go ye into all the world, and preach the gospel to every creature.[16] He that believeth and is baptized shall be saved; but he that believeth not shall be damned.[17] **And these signs shall follow them that believe**; In my name shall they cast out devils; they shall speak with new tongues;[18] They shall take up serpents; and if they drink any deadly thing, it shall not hurt them; they shall lay hands on the sick, and they shall recover.

Matthew 2:1-11-Now when Jesus was born in Bethlehem of Judaea in the days of Herod the king, behold, **there came wise men from the east to Jerusalem,** Saying, Where is he that is born King of the Jews? for we have seen his star in the east, and are come to worship him...When they had heard the king, they departed; and, lo, the star, which they saw in the east, went before them, till it came and stood over **where the young child was**. When they saw the star, they rejoiced with exceeding great joy. And when they were come **into the house, they saw the young child** with Mary his mother, and fell down, and worshipped him: and when they had opened their treasures, they presented unto him gifts; gold, and frankincense and myrrh.

Matthew 6:33-[31] Therefore take no thought, saying, What shall we eat? or, What shall we drink? or, Wherewithal shall we be clothed? [32] (For after all these things do the Gentiles seek:) for your heavenly Father knows that ye have need of all these things.[33] **But seek ye first the kingdom of God, and his righteousness; and all these things shall be added unto you.**

Matthew 7:18-22-Beware of **false prophets**, which come to you in sheep's clothing, but inwardly they are ravening wolves.[16] Ye shall know them **by their fruits**. Do men gather grapes of thorns, or figs of thistles?[17] Even so every good tree brings forth good fruit; but a corrupt tree brings forth evil fruit.[18] A good tree cannot bring forth evil fruit, neither can a corrupt tree bring forth good fruit.[19] Every tree that brings not forth good fruit is hewn down, and cast into the fire. Wherefore by their fruits ye shall know them. Not every one that says unto me, Lord, Lord, shall enter into the kingdom of heaven; but he that doeth the will of my Father which is in heaven. **Many will say to me in that day, Lord, Lord, have we not prophesied in thy name? and in thy name have cast out devils? and in thy name done many wonderful works? [23] And then will I profess unto them, I never knew you: depart from me, ye that work iniquity.**

Matthew 24:7, For nation shall rise against nation, and kingdom against kingdom: and there shall be famines, and pestilences, and earthquakes, in divers places. **All these are the beginning of sorrows.**

Matthew 24:15-When ye therefore shall see the **abomination of desolation, spoken of by Daniel the prophet, stand in the holy place**, (whoso reads, let him understand:) 16 then let them which be in Judæa flee into the mountains: 17 let him which is on the housetop not come down to take anything out of his house: 18 neither let him which is in the field return back to take his clothes. 19 And woe unto them that are with child, and to them that give suck in those days! 20 But pray ye that your flight be not in the winter, neither on the Sabbath day: 21 for then shall be **great tribulation**, such as was not since the beginning of the world to this time, no, nor ever shall be. 23 Then if any man shall say unto you, Lo, here is Christ, or there; believe it not. 24 For there shall arise false Christs, and false prophets, and shall show great signs and wonders; insomuch that, if it were possible, they shall deceive the very elect. 25 Behold, I have told you before. 26 Wherefore if they shall say unto you, Behold, he is in the desert; go not forth: behold, he is in the secret chambers; believe it not. 27 For as the lightning cometh out of the east, and shines even unto the west; so shall also the coming of the Son of man be. 28 For wheresoever the carcase is, there will the eagles be gathered together.

Matthew 24:32-41 Now learn a parable of the **fig tree;** When his branch is yet tender, and puts forth leaves, ye know that summer is nigh: 33 so likewise ye, when ye shall see all these things, know that it is near, even at the doors. 34 **Truly I say unto you, this generation shall not pass, till all these things be fulfilled**. 35 Heaven and earth shall pass away, but my words shall not pass away. 36 But of that day and hour knows no man, no, not the angels of heaven, but my Father only.37 But as the days of Noah were, so shall also the coming of the Son of man be. 38 For as in the days that were before the flood they were **eating and drinking, marrying and giving in marriage, until the day that Noah entered into the ark,** 39 and knew not until the flood came, and took them all away; so shall also the coming of the Son of man be. 40 Then shall two be in the field; the one shall be taken, and the other left. 41 Two women shall be grinding at the mill; the **one shall be taken, and the other left. 42 Watch therefore: for ye know not what hour your Lord doth come.**

Matthew 25: Then shall the kingdom of heaven be likened unto ten virgins, which took their lamps, and went forth to meet the bridegroom. 2 **And five of them were wise, and five were foolish.** 3 They that were foolish took their lamps, and took no oil with them: 4 but the wise took oil in their vessels with their lamps. 5 While the bridegroom tarried, they all slumbered and slept. 6 And at midnight there was a cry made, Behold, the bridegroom cometh; go ye out to meet him. 7 Then all those virgins arose, and trimmed their lamps. 8 And the foolish said unto the wise, Give us of your oil; for our lamps are gone out. 9 But the wise answered, saying, Not so; lest there be not enough for us and you: but go ye rather to them that sell, and buy for yourselves. 10 And while they went to buy, the bridegroom came; and **they that were ready went in with him to the marriage: and the door was shut.** 11 Afterward came also the other virgins, saying, Lord, Lord, open to us. 12 But he answered and said, Verily I say unto you, I know you not. 13 **Watch therefore, for ye know neither the day nor the hour wherein the Son of man cometh.**

Micah 5:2-2 But thou, **Bethlehem** Ephratah, though thou be little among the thousands of Judah, yet out of thee shall he come forth unto me that is to be **ruler in Israel; whose goings forth have**

been from of old, from everlasting.

Micah 7: [1] Woe is me! for I am as when they have gathered the summer fruits, as the grape gleanings of the vintage: there is no cluster to eat: my soul desired the firstripe fruit. [2] The **good man is perished** out of the earth: [*translated here as "perished", the Hebrew "abad" means to "wander away" or "lose ones' self". This could be the perspective of those who remain on the earth after the rapture. They will see the believers who are missing as simply lost or wandered away.*] and **there is none upright among men they all lie in wait for blood; they hunt every man his brother with a net.** [*At the very beginning of tribulation there is no one righteous on earth as those who remain on the earth don't receive Messiah until they hear the two witnesses whom God will send to preach Jesus. Notice the allusion to the Rapture of the church ("gathering of the first fruits") before the statement "none upright among men." James 1:18 states that Christians are considered "firstfruits." As long as the Church is on the earth, there is "upright among men." After the Rapture, there will be no righteous on the earth.*] [3] That they may do evil with both hands earnestly, the prince asks, and the judge asks for a reward; and the great man, he utters his mischievous desire: so they wrap it up. [4] The best of them is as a brier: the most upright is sharper than a thorn hedge: the day of thy watchmen and thy visitation cometh; now shall be their perplexity. [5] **Trust ye not in a friend, put ye not confidence in a guide: keep the doors of thy mouth from her that lies in thy bosom. [6] For the son dishonors the father, the daughter rises up against her mother, the daughter in law against her mother in law; a man's enemies are the men of his own house.** [7] Therefore I will look unto the LORD; I will wait for the God of my salvation: my God will hear me. [8] Rejoice not against me, O mine enemy: when I fall, I shall arise; when I sit in darkness, the LORD shall be a light unto me. [9] I will bear the **indignation of the LORD** *[God's wrath during Jacob's Trouble]*, because I have sinned against him, until he plead my cause, and execute judgment for me: he will bring me forth to the light, and I shall behold his righteousness.

Nahum 1:2-God is jealous, and the Lord revenges; the Lord revenges, and is furious; the **Lord will take vengeance on his adversaries, and**

Numbers 14: How long shall I bear with this evil congregation, which murmur against me? I have heard the murmurings of the children of Israel, which they murmur against me. 28 Say unto them, As truly as I live, says the Lord, as ye have spoken in mine ears, so will I do to you: 29 your carcasses shall fall in this wilderness; and all that were numbered of you, according to **your whole number, from twenty years old and upward,** which have murmured against me, 30 doubtless ye shall not come into the land, concerning which I swore to make you dwell therein, save Caleb the son of Jephunneh, and Joshua the son of Nun. 31 But your little ones, which ye said should be a prey, them will I bring in, and they shall know the land which ye have despised. 32 But as for you, your carcasses, they shall fall in this wilderness. 33 And your children shall wander in the wilderness forty years, and bear your whoredoms, until your carcasses be wasted in the wilderness. 34 After the number of the days in which ye searched the land, even forty days, each day for a year, shall ye bear your iniquities, even forty years, and ye shall know my breach of promise.

Philippians 3:20, 21-For our conversation is in heaven; from whence also we look for the Savior, the Lord Jesus Christ: **Who shall change our vile body, that it may be fashioned like unto his glorious body,** according to the working whereby he is able even to subdue all things unto himself.

Psalm 16:11-11 Thou wilt show me the path of life: **in thy presence is fullness of joy**; at thy right hand there are pleasures for evermore.

Psalm 22:16-18 For dogs have compassed me: the assembly of the wicked have inclosed me: **they pierced my hands and my feet.** 17 I may tell all my bones: they look and stare upon me. 18 **They part my garments among them, and cast lots upon my vesture.**

Psalm 90:10-The days of our years are **threescore years and ten; and if by reason of strength they be fourscore years,** yet is their strength labor and sorrow; for it is soon cut off, and we fly away.

Psalm 91: "**He that dwells in the secret place of the Most High shall abide under the shadow of the Almighty. I will say of the LORD, He is my refuge and my fortress: my God; in Him will I trust.** Surely He shall deliver thee from the snare of the fowler, and from the noisome pestilence. He shall cover thee with his feathers, and under His wings shall thou trust: His truth shall be thy shield and buckler. Thou shall not be afraid for the terror by night; nor for the arrow that flies by day; Nor for the pestilence that walks in darkness; nor for the destruction that wastes at noonday. **A thousand shall fall at thy side, and ten thousand at thy right hand; but it shall not come nigh thee.** Only with thine eyes shall thou behold and see the reward of the wicked. Because thou hast made the LORD, which is my refuge, even the most High, thy habitation; **There shall no evil befall thee, neither shall any plague come nigh thy dwelling. For He shall give His angels charge over thee, to keep thee in all thy ways.** They shall bear thee up in their hands, lest thou dash thy foot against a stone. Thou shall tread upon the lion and adder: the young lion and the dragon shall thou trample under feet. Because he hath set his love upon Me, therefore will I deliver him: I will set him on high, because he hath known My name [Jesus]. He shall call upon Me, and I will answer him: I will be with him in trouble; I will deliver him, and honor him. With long life will I satisfy him, and show him My salvation.

Revelation 2:[1] Unto the angel of the church of **Ephesus** write; These things saith he that holdeth the seven stars in his right hand, who walketh in the midst of the seven golden candlesticks; [2] I know thy works, and thy labour, and thy patience, and how thou canst not bear them which are evil: and thou hast tried them which say they are apostles, and are not, and hast found them liars: [3] And hast borne, and hast patience, and for my name's sake hast laboured, and hast not fainted. [4] Nevertheless I have somewhat against thee, because thou hast left thy first love. [5] Remember therefore from whence thou art fallen, and repent, and do the first works; or else I will come unto thee quickly, and will remove thy candlestick out of his place, except thou repent. [6] But this thou hast, that thou hatest the deeds of the Nicolaitans, which I also hate. [7] He that hath an ear, let him hear what the Spirit saith unto the churches; To him that overcometh will I give to eat of the tree of life, which is in the midst of the paradise of God. [8] And unto the angel of the church in **Smyrna** write; These things saith the first and the last, which was dead, and is alive; [9] I know thy works, and tribulation, and poverty, (but thou art rich) and I know the blasphemy of them which say they are Jews, and are not, but are the synagogue of Satan. [10] Fear none of those things which thou shalt suffer: behold, **the devil shall cast some of you into prison**, that ye may be tried; and ye shall have tribulation ten days: be thou faithful unto death, and I will give thee a crown of life. [11] He that hath an ear, let him hear what the Spirit saith unto the churches; He that overcomes shall not be hurt of the second death. [12] And to the angel of the church in **Pergamos** write; These things saith he which hath the sharp sword with two edges; [13] I know thy works, and where thou dwellest, even where Satan's seat is: and thou holdest fast my name, and hast not denied my faith, even in those days wherein Antipas was my faithful martyr, who was slain among you, where Satan dwelleth. [14] But I have a few things against thee, because thou hast there them that hold the doctrine of Balaam, who taught Balac to cast a stumblingblock before the children of Israel, to eat things sacrificed unto idols, and to commit fornication. [15] So hast thou also them that hold the doctrine of the Nicolaitans, which thing I hate. [16] Repent; or else I will come unto thee quickly, and will fight against them with the sword of my mouth. [17] He that hath an ear, let him hear what the Spirit saith unto the churches; To him that overcometh will I give to eat of the hidden manna, and will give him a white stone, and in the stone a new name written, which no man knoweth saving he that receiveth it. [18] And unto the angel of the church in **Thyatira** write; These things saith the Son of God, who hath his eyes like unto a flame of fire, and his feet are like fine brass; [19] I know thy works, and charity, and service, and faith, and thy patience, and thy works; and the last to be more than the first. [20] Notwithstanding I have a few things against thee, because thou sufferest that woman **Jezebel, which calleth herself a prophetess, to teach and to seduce my servants to commit fornication, and to eat things sacrificed unto idols.** [*"Jezebel" is equated with false religion joined with the true worship of God, as King Ahab allowed in Israel. There are occult New Age practices among some Christians-meditation, and emphasis on spiritual experiences of soul travel and other occult practices that have been welcomed into some church circles...there are deceiving spirits associated with it that Jesus condemns.*] [21] And I gave her space to repent of her fornication; and she repented not. [22] Behold, I will **cast her into a bed, and them that commit adultery with her into great tribulation, <u>except they repent of their deeds.</u>** [23] And I will kill her children with death; and all the churches shall know that I am he which searcheth the reins and hearts: and I will give unto every one of you according to your works. [24] But unto you I say, and unto the rest in Thyatira, as many as have not this doctrine, and which have not known the depths of Satan, as they speak; I will put upon you none other burden. [25] But that which ye have already hold fast till I come. [26] And he **that overcometh, and keepeth my works unto the end, to him will I give power over the nations: [27] And he shall rule them with a rod of iron; as the vessels of a potter shall they be broken to shivers**: even as I received of my Father. [28] And I will give him the morning star. [29] He that hath an ear, let him hear what the Spirit saith unto the churches.

Revelation 3:[1] And unto the angel of the church in **Sardis** write; These things says he that has the seven Spirits of God, and the seven stars; I know thy works, that thou hast a name that thou live, and art dead. [2] Be watchful, and strengthen the things which remain, that are ready to die: for I have not found thy works perfect before God. [3] Remember therefore how thou hast received and heard, and hold fast, and repent. If therefore thou shalt not watch, I will come on thee as a thief, and thou shalt not know what hour I will come upon thee. [4] Thou hast a few names even in Sardis which have not defiled their garments; and they shall walk with me in white: for they are worthy. [5] He that overcomes, the same shall be clothed in white raiment; and I will not blot out his name out of the book of life, but I will confess his name before my Father, and before his angels. [6] He that hath an ear, let him hear what the Spirit says unto the churches. [7] And to the angel of the church in **Philadelphia** write; These things says he that is holy, he that is true, he that hath the key of David, he that **opens, and no man shuts**; and shuts, and no man opens; [8] I know thy works: behold, I have set before thee an **open door**, and no man can shut it: for thou hast a little strength, and hast kept my word, and hast not denied my name. [9] Behold, I will make them of the synagogue of Satan, which say they are Jews, and are not, but do lie; behold, I will make them to come and worship before thy feet, and to know that I have loved thee. [10] *Because thou hast kept the word of my patience, I also will keep thee from the hour of temptation, which shall come upon all the world, to try them that dwell upon the earth*. [11] Behold, I come quickly: hold that fast which thou hast, that no man take thy crown. [12] Him that overcometh will I make a pillar in the temple of my God, and he shall go no more out: and I will write upon him the name of my God, and the name of the city of my God, which is new Jerusalem, which cometh down out of heaven from my God: and I will write upon him my new name. [13] He that hath an ear, let him hear what the Spirit saith unto the churches.26 and he that overcomes, and keeps my works unto the end, to him will I give power over the nations: 27 and **he shall rule them with a rod of iron;** as the vessels of a potter shall they be broken to shivers: even as I received of my Father. [14] And unto the angel of the church of the **Laodiceans** write; These things saith the Amen, the faithful and true witness, the beginning of the creation of God; [15] I know thy works, that thou art neither cold nor hot: I would thou wert cold or hot. [16] So then because thou art lukewarm, and neither cold nor hot, I will spue thee out of my mouth. [17] Because thou sayest, I am rich, and increased with goods, and have need of nothing; and knowest not that thou art wretched, and miserable, and poor, and blind, and naked: [18] I counsel thee to buy of me gold tried in the fire, that thou mayest be rich; and white raiment, that thou mayest be clothed, and that the shame of thy nakedness do not appear; and anoint thine eyes with eye salve, that thou mayest see. [19] As many as I love, I rebuke and chasten: be zealous therefore, and repent. [20] **Behold, I stand at the door, and knock: if any man hear my voice, and open the door, I will come in to him, and will sup with him, and he with me.** [21] To him that overcometh will I grant to sit with me in my throne, even as I also overcame, and am set down with my Father in his throne. [22] He that hath an ear, let him hear what the Spirit saith unto the churches.

Revelation 4:1 After this I looked, and, behold, a <u>door was opened in heaven</u>: and the first voice which I heard was as it were of a **trumpet** talking with me; which said, **Come up hither,** and I will show thee things which must be hereafter.

Revelation 6:7- And when he had opened the fourth seal, I heard the voice of the fourth beast say, Come and see. 8 And I looked, and behold a pale horse: and his name that sat on him was **Death,** and Hell followed with him. And power was given unto them over **the fourth part of the earth, to kill with sword, and with hunger, and with death, and with the beasts of the earth.**

Revelation 7:2-8-And I saw another angel ascending from the east, having the seal of the living God: and he cried with a loud voice to the four angels, to whom it was given to hurt the earth and the sea, 3 saying, Hurt not the earth, neither the sea, nor the trees, till we have **sealed the servants of our God** in their foreheads. 4 And I heard the number of them which were sealed: and there were sealed **an hundred and forty and four thousand of all the tribes of the children of Israel.** 5 Of the tribe of Juda were sealed twelve thousand. Of the tribe of Reuben were sealed twelve thousand. Of the tribe of Gad were sealed twelve thousand. 6 Of the tribe of Aser were sealed twelve thousand. Of the tribe of Nepthalim were sealed twelve thousand. Of the tribe of Manasses were sealed twelve thousand. 7 Of the tribe of Simeon were sealed twelve thousand. Of the tribe of Levi were sealed twelve thousand. Of the tribe of Issachar were sealed twelve thousand. 8 Of the tribe of Zabulon were sealed twelve thousand. Of the tribe of Joseph were sealed twelve thousand. Of the tribe of Benjamin were sealed twelve thousand.

Revelation 9:18- 18 By these three was **the third part of men killed**, by the fire, and by the smoke, and by the brimstone, which issued out of their mouths.

Revelation 12:5-12 And there appeared a great wonder in heaven; a **woman clothed with the sun, and the moon under her feet, and upon her head a crown of twelve stars:** 2 and she being with child cried, travailing in birth, and pained to be delivered. 3 And there appeared another wonder in heaven; and behold a great red dragon, having seven heads and ten horns, and seven crowns upon his heads. 4 And his tail drew the third part of the stars of heaven, and did cast them to the earth: and the dragon stood before the woman which was ready to be delivered, for to devour her child as soon as it was born. 5 And she brought forth a man child, who was to rule all nations with a rod of iron: and her **child was caught up unto God**, and to his throne. 6 And the woman fled into the wilderness, where she hath a place prepared of God, that they should feed her there a thousand two hundred and threescore days...13 And when the dragon saw that he was cast unto the earth, he persecuted the woman which brought forth the man child. 14 And to the **woman were given two wings of a great eagle, that she might fly into the wilderness, into her place, where she is nourished for a time, and times, and half a time, from the face of the serpent.**

Revelation 13:1 And I beheld another beast coming up out of the earth; and he had two **horns like a lamb, and he spoke as a dragon**. [The Lamb represents Christ, the Lamb of God, but the beast is a false Christ... he speaks on behalf of the devil-dragon.] 12 And he exercises all the power of the first beast before him, and causes the earth and them which dwell therein to worship the first beast, who's deadly wound was healed. 13 And he doeth great wonders, so that he makes fire come down from heaven on the earth in the sight of men, 14 and deceives them that dwell on the earth by the means of those miracles which he had power to do in the sight of the beast; saying to them that dwell on the earth, that they should make an image to the beast, which had the wound by a sword, and did live. 15 And he had power to give life unto the image of the beast, that the image of the beast should both speak, **and cause that as many as would not worship the image of the beast <u>should be killed</u>. 16 And he causes all, both small and great, rich and poor, free and bond, to receive a mark in their right hand, or in their foreheads: 17 and that no man might buy or sell, save he that had the mark, or the name of the beast, or the number of his name. 18** Here is wisdom. Let him that hath understanding count the number of the beast: for it is the number of a man; and his number is Six hundred threescore and six.

Revelation 17: [1] And there came one of the seven angels which had the seven vials, and talked with me, saying unto me, Come hither; I will show unto thee the judgment of the great whore that **sits upon many waters:** [2] With whom the kings of the earth have committed fornication, and the inhabitants of the earth have been made drunk with the wine of her fornication. [3] So he carried me away in the spirit into the wilderness: and I saw a woman sit upon a scarlet colored beast, full of names of blasphemy, having seven heads and ten horns. [4] And the woman was arrayed in purple and scarlet color, and decked with gold and precious stones and pearls, having a golden cup in her hand full of abominations and filthiness of her fornication: [5] And upon her forehead was a name written, MYSTERY, BABYLON THE GREAT, THE MOTHER OF HARLOTS AND ABOMINATIONS OF THE EARTH. [6] And **I saw the woman <u>drunken with the blood of the saints, and with the blood of the martyrs of Jesus:</u>** and when I saw her, I wondered with great admiration. [7] And the angel said unto me, Wherefore didst thou marvel? I will tell thee the mystery of the woman, and of the beast that carries her, which hath the seven heads and ten horns. [8] The beast that thou saw was, and is not; and shall ascend out of the bottomless pit, and go into perdition: and they that dwell on the earth shall wonder, whose names were not written in the book of life from the foundation of the world, when they behold the beast that was, and is not, and yet is. [9] And here is the mind which hath wisdom. The **seven heads are seven mountains, on which the woman sits**. [10] And there are seven kings: five are fallen, and one is, and the other is not yet come; and when he cometh, he must continue a short space. [11] And the beast that was, and is not, even he is the eighth, and is of the seven, and goes into perdition. [12] And the ten horns which thou saw are ten kings, which have received no kingdom as yet; but receive power as kings one hour with the beast. [13] These have one mind, and shall give their power and strength unto the beast. [14] These shall make war with the Lamb, and the Lamb shall overcome them: for he is Lord of lords, and King of kings: and they that are with him are called, and chosen, and faithful. **[15] And he says unto me, The waters which thou saw, where the whore sits, are peoples, and multitudes, and nations, and tongues.** [16] And the ten horns which thou saw upon the beast, these shall hate the whore, and shall make her desolate and naked, and shall eat her flesh, and burn her with fire. [17] For God hath put in their hearts to fulfil his will, and to agree, and give their kingdom unto the beast, until the words of God shall be fulfilled. [18] And the woman which thou saw is that great city, which reigns over the kings of the earth.

Rev.18: [1] And after these things I saw another angel come down from heaven, having great power; and the earth was lightened with his glory. [2] And he cried mightily with a strong voice, saying, **Babylon the great is fallen, is fallen**, and is become the habitation of devils, and the hold of every foul spirit, and a cage of every unclean and hateful bird. [3] For all nations have drunk of the wine of the wrath of her fornication, and the kings of the earth have committed fornication with her, and the merchants of the earth are waxed rich through the abundance of her delicacies. [4] And I heard another voice from heaven, saying, **Come out of her, my people, that ye be not partakers of her sins, and that ye receive not of her plagues. [5] For her sins have reached unto heaven, and God hath remembered her iniquities**. [6] *[The identity of end-time "Babylon" has been debated. Of course there is the literal, historic Babylon, but in the case of the "Babylon" that God judges in the last days, it is* *evident that it refers to a symbolic "Babylon" since the literal city no longer exists as a world power. "Mystery Babylon" is definitely referring to the* **Roman Catholic church that sits on the Seven Hills of Rome.** *It is a religious system with a long history. Rome is the very city responsible for shedding the blood of the martyrs and the apostles. Though Mystery Babylon refers to the Roman Catholic Church, but it also can have other spiritual applications. Many prophetic scriptures have a two-fold application and fulfillment (e.g., abomination of desolation referred both to Antiochus Ephiphanes and the anti-Christ.) The "Babylon" referred to in Jeremiah 51 refers to the literal Babylon when God judges it in 539 B.C. by Cyrus the Mede. Some have interpreted the United States as also being a type of Babylon that will be judged of God, citing Jeremiah 51 and Isaiah 18 & 47. It is very possible—even likely—that the United States is alluded to (especially in Isaiah 18.) However, the admonition to "come out of her My people" is not so much referring to fleeing a geographic place, but a spiritual place: "come out" of the false religious, idolatrous system of the world. Mass emigration of millions of people to flee from the United States is not feasible. Those who stay close to the Lord will be kept safe even in the midst of catastrophic natural disasters and terror attacks that will likely befall the USA even before the Rapture. Jesus said to "go into all the world and preach the Gospel to every creature"...* including the United States. Though the United States may very well be judged for turning away from God's Holy standards of righteousness, those who are His can rest assured that He will protect and provide for His own if they seek first the Kingdom of God. The fulfillment of Mystery Babylon is during the tribulation period, and refers to the false religious system seated in Rome: *"Reward her even as she rewarded you, and double unto her double according to her works: in the cup which she hath filled fill to her double. [7] How much she hath glorified herself, and lived deliciously, so much torment and sorrow give her: for she says in her heart, I sit a queen, and am no widow, and shall see no sorrow. [8] Therefore shall her plagues come in one day, death, and mourning, and famine; and she shall be utterly burned with fire: for strong is the Lord God who judges her. [9] And the kings of the earth, who have committed fornication and lived* deliciously with her, shall bewail her, and lament for her, when they shall see the smoke of her burning, [10] Standing afar off or the fear of her torment, saying, Alas, alas, that great city Babylon, that mighty city! for in one hour is thy judgment come. [11] And the merchants of the earth shall weep and mourn over her; for no man buys their merchandise any more: [12] **The merchandise of gold, and silver, and precious stones, and of pearls, and fine linen, and purple, and silk, and scarlet, and all thyine wood, and all manner vessels of ivory, and all manner vessels of most precious wood, and of brass, and iron, and marble, [13] And cinnamon, and odors, and ointments, and frankincense, and wine, and oil, and fine flour, and wheat, and beasts, and sheep, and horses, and chariots, and slaves, and <u>souls of men</u>**. [14] And the fruits that thy soul lusted after are departed from thee, and all things which were dainty and goodly are departed from thee, and thou shalt find them no more at all. [15] The merchants of these things, which were made rich by her, shall stand afar off for the fear of her torment, weeping and wailing, [16] And saying, Alas, alas, that great city, that was clothed in fine linen, and purple, and scarlet, and decked with gold, and precious stones, and pearls! [17] For in one hour so great riches is come to nought. And every shipmaster, and all the company in ships, and sailors, and as many as trade by sea, stood afar off, [18] And cried when they saw the smoke of her burning, saying, What city is like unto this great city! [19] And they cast dust on their heads, and cried, weeping and wailing, saying, Alas, alas, that great city, wherein were made rich all that had ships in the sea by reason of her costliness! for in one hour is she made desolate. [20] **Rejoice over her, thou heaven, and ye <u>holy apostles and prophets;</u> for God hath avenged you on her**. [21] And a mighty angel took up a stone like a great millstone, and cast it into the sea, saying, Thus with violence shall that great city Babylon be thrown down, and shall be found no more at all. [22] And the voice of harpers, and musicians, and of pipers, and trumpeters, shall be heard no more at all in thee; and no craftsman, of whatsoever craft he be, shall be found any more in thee; and the sound of a millstone shall be heard no more at all in thee; [23] And the light of a candle shall shine no more at all in thee; and the voice of the bridegroom and of the bride shall be heard no more at all in thee: for thy merchants were the great men *of the earth; for by thy sorceries were all nations deceived. [24] And in her was found the blood of prophets, and of saints, and of all that were slain upon the earth."*

Note: Historically, no apostles were killed by the United States of America. They were all martyred by the powers of Rome. "Mystery Babylon" definitely refers to the Roman Catholic Church. Of course, there was certainly the historic fact that God did judge the literal city of Babylon and allowed for the Medes and Persians to overtake it in 539 B.C. However, the extent of that judgment has never been fully fulfilled (i.e., complete, surprise desolation so that it would never be inhabited again.) The take-over by the Medes & Persians and subsequent dominating powers over that area did not render it fully uninhabitable. Today the city of Hillah in Iraq sits on the site of Babylon and bricks from the ancient city were used to build Hillah. Jeremiah 50, 51, and Isaiah 14, 18, and 47 all refer to Babylon or the daughter of Babylon and describe the judgment thereof. Some of the judgment has been fulfilled, and some is directed to futurist "Babylon." Some think the ancient city has to be rebuilt and somehow will become the economic power of the world again. However, the writer contends that these prophecies have other possible futuristic fulfillments including the "daughter of Babylon" as a symbol for the United States. The judgment of God could be precipitated by the national trend to replace traditional moral standards of the God of the Bible with the gods of materialism and pleasure and immorality. New York City is the seat of the United State's economy and could be that which is described as the "daughter of Babylon" that is judged in the last days. This does not preclude the Roman Catholic Church as still being judged during the Great Tribulation. The writer contends that it is not necessarily an "either/or" interpretation (either the United States or the Roman Catholic church) but can be futuristically fulfilled in both: The United States being judged before the tribulation—"daughter of Babylon," and the Roman Catholic church (Mystery Babylon the Great) being judged toward the end of the tribulation. A two-fold futuristic fulfillment of prophecy has definite Biblical precedence (e.g., Antiochus Epiphanes and the antichrist are BOTH legitimate fulfillments of the "Abomination of Desolation" prophecies, with the former only partially fulfilling it in 167 B.C., whereas the latter will be the complete fulfillment during the Great Tribulation.) The United States can especially be construed in Isaiah 18 and 47, as well as parts of Jeremiah 51. However, the Revelation 18 "Mystery Babylon" is definitely fulfilled in the Roman Catholic church. The specific breakdown of the afore-mentioned scriptural fulfillments is for another time and another book.) The "come out of her My people" refers to coming out of the corrupt religious pseudo-christian system of the Catholic church, and also can be construed as an ad-monition for believers not to be caught up with the spirit of the world (lust of the eyes, lust of the flesh, and pride of life) so prevalent in the United States of America. A pre-tribulation judgment of the United States would certainly help to establish the EU as the bastion of power from which the antichrist will gain world domination. Therefore, "Babylon" can be BOTH the economic system of America before the Great Tribulation and the false religious Roman system, that provides the antichrist a false prophet pope during the tribulation.

Revelation 19:7-20 "Let us be glad and rejoice, and give honor to him: for the marriage of the Lamb is come, and **his wife** hath made herself ready." 8 And to her was granted that she should be arrayed in **fine linen, clean and white: for the fine linen is the righteousness of saints.** 9 And he says unto me, Write, Blessed are they which are called unto the marriage supper of the Lamb. And he says unto me, These are the true sayings of God. 10 And I fell at his feet to worship him. And he said unto me, See thou do it not: I am thy fellow servant, and of thy brethren that have the testimony of Jesus: worship God: for the testimony of Jesus is the spirit of prophecy.11 And I saw heaven opened, and behold a white horse; and he that sat upon him was called Faithful and True, and in righteous- ness he doth judge and make war. 12 His eyes were as a flame of fire, and on his head were many crowns; and he had a name written, that no man knew, but he himself. 13 And he was clothed with a vesture dipped in blood: and his name is called The

Word of God. 14 **And the armies which were in heaven followed him upon white horses, clothed in fine linen, white and clean.** 15 And out of his mouth goes a sharp sword, that with it he should smite the nations: and he shall rule them with a rod of iron: and he treads the winepress of the fierceness and wrath of Almighty God. 16 And he hath on his vesture and on his thigh a name written, KING OF KINGS, AND LORD OF LORDS.17 And I saw an angel standing in the sun; and he cried with a loud voice, saying to all the fowls that fly in the midst of heaven, Come and gather yourselves together unto the supper of the great God; 18 that ye may eat the flesh of kings, and the flesh of captains, and the flesh of mighty men, and the flesh of horses, and of them that sit on them, and the flesh of all men, both free and bond, both small and great. 19 And I saw the beast, and the kings of the earth, and their armies, gathered together to make war against him that sat on the horse, and against his army. 20 And the beast was taken, and with him the false prophet that wrought miracles before him, with which he deceived them that had received the mark of the beast, and them that worshipped his image. These both were cast alive into a lake of fire burning with brimstone.

Revelation 20-And I saw the dead, small and great, stand before God; and the books were opened: and another book was opened, which is the book of life: and the dead were judged out of those things which were written in the books, according to their works. And the sea gave up the dead which were in it; and death and hell delivered up the dead which were in them: and they were judged every man according to their works. And death and hell were cast into the lake of fire. This is the second death. **And whosoever was not found written in the book of life was cast into the lake of fire.**

Romans 3:23- For **all have sinned, and come short of the glory of God;**

Romans 6:23-For **the wages of sin is death;** but the gift of God is eternal life through Jesus Christ our Lord.

Romans 11:25 For I would not, brethren, that ye should be ignorant of this mystery, lest ye should be wise in your own conceits; *that blindness in part is happened to Israel,* **until the full- ness of the Gentiles be come in. 26 And so all Israel shall be saved:** as it is written, There shall come out of Sion the Deliverer, and shall turn away ungodliness from Jacob: 27 for this is my covenant unto them, when I shall take away their sins.

Song of Solomon 2:10-My beloved spoke, and said unto me, *Rise up, my love, my fair one, and come away...13-the fig tree* puts forth her green figs, and the vines with the tender grape give a good smell. Arise, my love, my fair one, and come away.

Zechariah 11:12, 13 And I said unto them, If ye think good, give me my price; and if not, forbear. So they weighed for my price **thirty pieces of silver.** And the Lord said unto me, **Cast it unto the potter**: a goodly price that I was priced at of them. **And I took the thirty pieces of silver, and cast them to the potter in the house of the Lord.**

Zechariah 12:10- And I will pour upon the house of David, and upon the inhabitants of Jerusalem, the spirit of grace and of sup- plications: and **they shall look upon Me whom they have pierced**, and they shall mourn for him, as one mourns for his only son, and shall be in bitterness for him, as one that is in bitterness for his firstborn.

Zechariah 13:2-6-And it shall come to pass in that day *[when the nation of Israel recognizes the true Messiah Jesus toward the end of the seven year tribulation]*, says the Lord of hosts, that I will cut off the names of the idols out of the land, and they shall be no more remembered: and **also I will cause the prophets and the unclean spirit to pass out of the land.** And it shall come to pass, that when any shall yet prophesy, then his father and his mother that begat him shall say unto him, 'You shall not live, for you speak lies in the Name of the Lord': and his father and his mother that begat him shall thrust him through when he prophesies. And it shall come to pass in that day, that **the prophets shall be ashamed every one of his vision,** when he hath prophesied; neither shall they wear a rough garment to deceive: But **he shall say, 'I am no prophet**, I am a husbandman; for man taught me to keep cattle from my youth. And one shall say unto him, '<u>what are these wounds in thine</u> <u>hands? Then he shall answer, 'those with which I was</u> <u>wounded in the house of my friends.'</u>

Zechariah 14: Then shall the Lord go forth, and fight against those nations, as when he fought in the day of battle. 4 And his feet shall stand in that day upon the mount of Olives, which is before Jerusalem on the east, and the mount of Olives shall cleave in the midst thereof toward the east and toward the west, and there shall be a very great valley; and half of the mountain shall remove toward the north, and half of it toward the south. 5 And ye shall flee to the valley of the mountains; for the valley of the mountains shall reach unto Azal: yea, ye shall flee, like as ye fled from before the earthquake in the days of Uzziah king of Judah: and the **Lord my God shall** <u>come, and all the saints</u> <u>with thee.</u>